WORD MAGIC

ULICK O'CONNOR

WORD MAGIC

'We are such stuff as dreams are made on'

CURRACH
PRESS

First published in 2005 by
CURRACH PRESS
55A Spruce Avenue, Stillorgan Industrial Park, Blackrock,
Co Dublin, Ireland

www.currach.ie

1 3 5 4 2

Cover design by Anú Design
Origination by Currach Press
Printed by ColourBooks Ltd, Dublin

ISBN 1-85607-931-7

Acknowledgements

I would like to say how grateful I am to Terry Wogan for his foreword.
The *Evening Herald* have been most helpful in ensuring that each
week's contribution is given generous presentation in their columns.

Gerry O'Flaherty's help with editing of the manuscript has been
invaluable.

CONTENTS

FOREWORD

I love poetry; I can quote reams and staves of it, because, like my friend, Ulick, I learned it for exams in school These days, they'll tell you that's wrong, that you'll never learn to love anything you learn by rote. They're wrong, that's how you learn to love poetry, try reciting it to yourself, listening and finally, understanding. The cadences, the rhythms, the rhymes, the words — the beautiful words. With his eye for beauty and his love of words, Ulick O'Connor has selected well for your delight. I could have wished for some of my own favourites: Gray's 'Elegy', Robert Frost, even 'Adelstrop' but I am sure Ulick will get around to them, after all, there is so much richness to be found — and there's more than enough here to please every ear.

Recite these poems to yourself, they'll stay with you all your life.

Terry Wogan

INTRODUCTION

This selection is from a series contributed once a week to the *Evening Herald*. I choose a poem that I think would entertain the reader and add a short paragraph on the background of the poem and its author. I have in my mind a person sitting on top of a bus and hope he/she may experience the pleasure that can be got from a real poem.

There is no pattern underlying the choice of poems. I cast around at the beginning of the week and then decide on one that could bring a flash to the reader's mind.

I know that all the verses I have chosen here will not please every reader. But I do hope that many will experience that special delight brought to the mind by a true poem.

OSCAR WILDE
1854-1900

20/04/02

Just a hundred and five years ago this spring Oscar Wilde's first successful play *A Woman of No Importance* was an immediate hit on the West End. A lord of language Wilde could write poetry, novels, and talk as no one in English has ever done before or since. Yet his light was low in the 1950s and his prose languished in competition with Ernest Hemingway's muscular use of the semi-colon. In August 1954 on the centenary of his birth I stood outside the door of Wilde's house, 24 Westland Row, Dublin as Lennox Robinson the playwright unveiled a plaque, and Micheál MacLiammóir who was to help to revive Oscar's fame with his one man show, made an eloquent speech to a tiny crowd.

Now Oscar's back in the saddle again, up with his two fellow Dubliners: W. B. Yeats and James Joyce, who are top of the list as the best poet and prose writer of the twentieth century.

'Helas' is an almost perfect sonnet. Perhaps rhyming the word 'holiday' with 'virelay' is a little cheeky, but then Oscar could get away with it.

HELAS

To drift with every passion till my soul
Is a stringed lute on which all winds can play,
Is it for this that I have given away
Mine ancient wisdom, and austere control?
Methinks my life is a twice-written scroll
Scrawled over on some boyish holiday
With idle songs for pipe and virelay,
Which do but mar the secret of the whole.
Surely there was a time I might have trod
The sunlit heights, and from life's dissonance
Struck one clear chord to reach the ears of God:
Is that time dead? Lo ! with a little rod
I did but touch the honey of romance –
And must I lose a soul's inheritance?

SEUMAS O'SULLIVAN
1879-1958

27/04/02

A good poem should put you in touch with an experience stolen from time imprisoned in rhyme and rhythm. That is what 'A Piper' by Seumas O'Sullivan does. As you read it you almost hear the music coming off the page.

Seumas O'Sullivan who wrote it, was a chemist in Rathmines under his real name James Starkey. He, Oliver St John Gogarty, James Stephens and Padraic Colum were young poets who nestled under the wings of Yeats's patronage in the Golden Age of Irish literature at the start of the twentieth century. James Joyce was a pal, when he and Gogarty lived in the Martello Tower in Sandycove in 1904. When the usual Irish split came Seumas sided with Æ's (George Russell) group, and Gogarty with Yeats' who made an appallingly high handed remark when asked about the deserter Seumas O'Sullivan —

Why should a wild dog praise his fleas?

Seumas O'Sullivan went on to edit *The Dublin Magazine*, one of the best literary journals of the century anywhere, and married painter Estella Solomons who is one of the most underestimated portrait painters of our time. Buy her pictures if you see them around.

A PIPER

A piper came to our street today,
Set up, and tuned, and started to play,
And away, away, away on the tide
Of his music we started, on every side
Doors and windows were opened wide,
And men left down their work and came,
And women with petticoats coloured like flame,
And little bare feet that were blue with cold,
Went dancing back to the age of gold,
And all the world went gay went gay,
For half an hour in our street today.

JAMES STEPHENS
1883-1950

29/03/03

James Stephens was the J. K. Rowling of his day. When his fairy tale book *The Crock of Gold* came out in 1912, it sold many thousands and was translated into several languages. But Stephens was also a serious poet and story writer who built up a large following on the BBC, reciting his poems in one of the best voices for speaking verse ever heard. He was also a star conversationalist in London social circles, holding the floor at literary evenings of the great London hostesses, presently annoying the famous Lytton Strachey who simply couldn't see the point of this 'little gnome-like figure gassing away thirteen to the dozen'.

Educated at the Meath Protestant Industrial School for boys and working as a solicitor's clerk wasn't the best introduction to the magic world that little James created. But he had a habit of being perpetually on the alert, and even walking on Sandymount strand when he picked up a shell, a poem magically wafted itself out of it —

I cannot tell you how it came or why, only that when it
did arrive it came well.

But the landscape that listening to the sounds in the shell brought up before Stephen's mind is a scary one, not the sun-kissed paradises that are advertised in the tourist brochures.

from THE SHELL

And then I pressed the shell
Close to my ear,
And listened well.

And straightway, like a bell,
Came low and clear
The slow, sad, murmur of far distant seas

Whipped by an icy breeze
Upon a shore
Wind-swept and desolate.

It was a sunless strand that never bore
The footprint of a man,
Nor felt the weight...

. . . .

And in the hush of waters was the sound
Of pebbles, rolling round;
For ever rolling, with a hollow sound:

And bubbling sea-weeds, as the waters go,
Swish to and fro
Their long cold tentacles of slimy grey:

. . . .

And waves that journeyed blind ...
And then I loosed my ear — Oh, it was sweet
To hear a cart go jolting down the street.

THOMAS MICHAEL KETTLE MP
1880-1916

4/05/02

Thomas Michael Kettle was in the trenches in France when he wrote this poem in the summer of 1916. Coming from an old Irish family with revolutionary connections, but believing that Home Rule was on the statute book, he had volunteered to fight in the British Army in the Great War on patriotic grounds. A brilliant conversationalist, a writer, and essayist and member of parliament, as a professor in University College Dublin he was adored by his students. When he was back on leave in Dublin in 1916 the rebellion broke out and he was heartbroken when his old friend and colleague in UCD, Thomas McDonagh, was executed as one of the leaders. Kettle went back to France where refusing a safe job behind the lines he asked to be sent straight to the Front and was killed at Guillemont on the Somme on 4 September 1916. A few days before, he wrote this fine poem to his daughter forged in the heat of disillusionment and battle, which I have to say is in the class of any written by the great English war poets, Rupert Brooke, Wilfred Owen or Isaac Rosenberg. I once met Betty with her mother Mary Kettle in their house in Charlemount Road. James Joyce had been in love with Mary (Emma Clery in *A Portrait of the Artist as a Young Man*) and I seemed to be looking at two figures snatched from time whose beauty had faded in front of one's eyes.

You can see Tom Kettle's fine bust by Albert Power any day in the centre of St Stephen's Green.

TO MY DAUGHTER BETTY,
THE GIFT OF GOD

In wiser days, my darling rosebud, blown
To beauty proud as was your mother's prime,
In that desired, delayed, incredible time,
You'll ask why I abandoned you, my own,
And the dear heart that was your baby throne,
To dice with death. And oh! They'll give you rhyme
And reason: some will call the thing sublime,
And some decry it in a knowing tone.
So here, while the mad guns curse overhead,
And tired men sigh with mud for couch and floor,
Know that we fools, now with the foolish dead,
Died not for flag, nor King, nor Emperor,
But for a dream, born in a herdsman's shed,
And for the secret Scripture of the poor.

THOMAS HOOD
1799-1845

17/05/02

Thomas Hood's father, who was a London bookseller, grew up surrounded by books. Later as editor of the *London Magazine,* Hood would publish famous writers like Charles Lamb, William Haslitt and Thomas de Quincy. It didn't seem to occur to him that he might himself be as good as those he was publishing. It wasn't until he was well on in life that he began to write poetry and to develop the gift that led to his verse being included in decent English poetry anthologies. His best known poem is 'Past and Present' with its simple but beautiful opening lines and note of sadness about vanished youth which alas reflected Hood's own life. He died aged forty-six after enduring a series of financial disasters as both publisher and magazine editor.

from PAST AND PRESENT

I remember, I remember
The house where I was born,
The little window where the sun
Came peeping in at morn;
He never came a wink too soon
Nor brought too long a day;
But now, I often wish the night
Had borne my breath away.

I remember, I remember
The roses, red and white,
The violets, and the lily-cups —
Those flowers made of light!
The lilacs where the robin built,
And where my brother set
The laburnum on his birthday, —
The tree is living yet!

I remember, I remember
The fir trees dark and high;
I used to think their slender tops
Were close against the sky:
It was a childish ignorance,
But now 'tis little joy
To know I'm farther off from Heaven
Than when I was a boy.

HILAIRE BELLOC
1870-1953

8/06/02

The trouble about Hilaire Belloc was that he wrote too much. He refused to make a living at anything else but writing and could churn out a biography almost in the same time as it could take another journalist to pen a long newspaper article. He had a knack of forecasting the wrong result in almost every battle he wrote about when he was a military commentator for *The Times* in the First World War. But he wrote wonderfully about travel and sailing in brilliant prose that will last. He was unexpectedly modern with his attacks on globalisation and the abuse of industrial and monetary power in a servile state.

Perhaps if he had had another trade instead of journalism the lamp of his poetry might have shone brighter. After all, T. S. Eliot refused to give up his job as a bank clerk while he was a world famous poet and Gerard Manley Hopkins only wrote his masterpieces in between lecturing and saying mass as a practising Jesuit. Either would have admired this poem by Belloc.

ON A SLEEPING FRIEND

Lady, when your lovely head
Droops to sink among the Dead
And the quiet places keep
You that so divinely sleep;
Then the dead shall blessed be
With a new solemnity,
For such beauty, so descending,
Pledges them that Death is ending.
Sleep your fill — but when you wake
Dawn shall over Lethe break.

FANNY PARNELL
1848-1882

11/05/02

Why does everyone forget the Parnell sisters when talking of their brother Charles? They grew up in Eccles Street, Dublin, with him and shared his love of Ireland. Fanny and Anna took charge of the Land League when their brother and Michael Davitt were doing a long stretch in Kilmainham Prison in the 1880s. They ostentatiously attended the trial of the Fenian O'Donovan Rossa for treason at Green Street, and Anna threw a rose into the dock as the judge was handing down his fearful fifteen-year sentence. Fanny was the one in the family who could get her own way with brother Charles. As children they used to play games of shooting down tin soldiers and one day after he had won she found that he had glued down some of the soldiers before the shooting started, and vowed she wouldn't be caught this way again. Fanny was very beautiful and a good poet, but she had frail health and died at thirty-four. Her poetry had a real vogue in America and was often compared with that of the poetess Julia Ward Howe the author of 'The Battle Hymn of the Republic'.

from AFTER DEATH

Shall mine eyes behold the glory, oh, my country?
Shall mine eyes behold the glory?
Or shall the darkness close around them ere the sun-blaze
Break at last upon thy story?

When the nations ope for thee their queenly circle,
As a new sweet sister hail thee,
Shall these lips be seal'd in callous death and silence,
That have known but to bewail thee?

Shall the ear be deaf that only loved thy praises,
When all men their tribute bring thee?
Shall the mouth be clay that sang thee in thy squalor,
When all poets' mouths shall sing thee?

I should turn and rend the cere-cloths round me—
Giant sinews I should borrow—
Crying 'Oh, my brothers, I have also loved her
In her loneliness and sorrow!

'Let me join with you the jubilant procession,
Let me chant with you her story;
Then, contented, I shall go back to the shamrocks,
Now mine eyes have seen her glory.'

JOHN BOYLE O'REILLY
1844-1890

1/06/02

When John Devoy, the Fenian organiser, met John Boyle O'Reilly in the 1860s he thought he was the handsomest man he had ever seen with his 'dark blue huzzar uniform and the buzby with its tossing plume set jauntily on his head'. They were meeting in Kilmainham next door to the barracks to plan the Fenian Rising where O'Reilly was a sergeant in the Huzzars. However a spy shopped O'Reilly and he was transported to Australia, but escaped in a whaling ship and ended up in Boston where he became a literary giant and editor of *The Boston Pilot* mixing as an equal with Oliver Wendell Holmes, John Greenleaf Whittier, Julia Ward Howe and others. Mrs Rose Kennedy once told me that John Boyle O'Reilly set the literary tone of the Boston of her childhood. His output was enormous: novels, articles, polemics, and running *The Boston Pilot,* in which he published the first poems of the young W. B. Yeats.

When Sir Arthur Quiller-Couch came to publish the best poems in English from 1250-1900 for his *Oxford Book of English Verse* he included 'A White Rose' by the former Tenth Huzzar and Fenian rebel John Boyle O'Reilly, who perhaps would have been surprised to have found himself immortalised alongside William Shakespeare, Lord Byron, Shelley and Tennyson.

A WHITE ROSE

The red rose whispers of passion,
And the white rose breathes of love;
O, the red rose is a falcon,
And the white rose is a dove.

But I send you a cream-white rosebud
With a flush on its petal tips;
For the love that is purest and sweetest
Has a kiss of desire on the lips.

LORD BYRON
1788-1824

15/06/02

Lord Byron was the first European pin-up. In France and Italy he was regarded as the greatest poet in English since Shakespeare. Back home he wasn't so popular because of his republican views and also because of goings on with his niece Augusta Leigh. He spent most of his later years in Venice, where he had the reputation of dividing his affection between the girls and gondoliers. Byron had achieved a vast body of verse before his death at thirty-six. Nothing daunted him. Despite his limp, he and Bob Tisdall from Tipperary (who won an Olympic gold medal in the hurdles in 1932) were the only students ever to have jumped up the twenty steps at the entrance to the dining hall in Trinity College, Cambridge in one leap. Byron died at Missonlonghi fighting for the freedom of the Greeks against the Turks.

When I heard just awhile ago that Byron's publishers John Murray were being taken over after more than two hundred and fifty years of family ownership, the one consolation was that the last book launched in the Byron room at 50 Albermarle Street, London was my own collection of *Diaries*, and the person who launched it for me holds the record number of tries for a British and Irish rugby team in South Africa.

from WE'LL GO NO MORE A ROVING

So, we'll go no more a-roving
So late into the night,
Though the heart be still as loving,
And the moon be still as bright.

For the sword outwears its sheath,
And the soul wears out the breast,
And the heart must pause to breathe
And love itself have rest.

Though the night was made for loving,
And the day returns too soon,
Yet we'll go no more a-roving
By the light of the moon.

ALAN SEEGER
1888-1916

22/06/02

Everyone knows who Pete Seegar, the singer, is. But who has heard of Alan Seeger? He was an upper class American who went to fight for France at the outbreak of the First World War, simply because he wanted to preserve French culture from the invading Germans. He wrote to his mother"

> It was only that the France, and especially the Paris, that I love shall not cease to be the glory and the beauty that they are, that I engaged.

He was killed in the summer of 1916 going over the top with the Foreign Legion of France enfiladed by six German machine guns in the attack on Belloy-en-Santerre. Seeger was a serious poet. One of his poems, 'I have a rendezvous with Death', is an almost perfect piece, capturing the mood of many high minded young English, German, French and American men who went out to fight for a cause they believed in but which turned out in the end to be an appalling and futile carnage fought on both sides simply to save decaying empires.

I HAVE A RENDEZVOUS WITH DEATH

I have a rendezvous with Death
At some disputed barricade,
When Spring comes back with rustling shade
And apple-blossoms fill the air —
I have a rendezvous with Death
When Spring brings back blue days and fair.

It may be he shall take my hand
And lead me into his dark land
And close my eyes and quench my breath —
It may be I shall pass him still.
I have a rendezvous with Death
On some scarred shape of battered hill
When Spring comes round again this year
And the first meadow-flowers appear.

God knows 'twere better to be deep
Pillowed in silk and scented down,
When Love throbs out in blissful sleep,
Pulse sighs to pulse and breath to breath,
Where hushed awakenings are dear ...
But I have a rendezvous with Death
At midnight in some flaming town,
When Spring trips North again this year,
And I to my pledged word am true,
I shall not fail that rendezvous.

GILBERT KEITH CHESTERTON
1872-1936

29/06/02

Nearly seventy years after his death G. K. Chesterton is having a come-back. He and Bernard Shaw in the Edwardian era anticipated the modern talk show with their brilliant public debates in Fleet Street which packed the aisles. The English loved him because of his Englishness and therefore listened to him when he told them that being English was not always the same as being good. He regarded fair play as an English trait and was incredibly fair minded when it came to Ireland.

> The Irish are the most powerful and practical world-combination with whom we can decide to be friends or foes.

Michael Collins was a fan and carried in his hip pocket a copy of Chesterton's famous novel, *The Napoleon of Notting Hill*, whose theme was revolution by London boroughs to seek independence from Central Authority. Chesterton was such an incredible all-rounder, pamphleteer, essayist, newspaper columnist and writer of best-seller detective stories that it's easy to forget how good a poet he is. His 'The Donkey' is a little masterpiece. GKC, always on the side of the underdog, sees Christ's triumphant entry into Jerusalem through the eyes of the sturdy little animal on whose back he rode.

THE DONKEY

When fishes flew and forests walk'd
And figs grew upon thorn,
Some moment when the moon was blood
Then surely I was born;

With monstrous head and sickening cry
And ears like errant wings,
The devil's walking parody
On all four-footed things.

The tatter'd outlaw of the earth,
Of ancient crooked will;
Starve, scourge, deride me: I am dumb,
I keep my secret still.

Fools! For I also had my hour;
One far fierce hour and sweet;
There was a shout about my ears,
And palms before my feet.

MICHAEL DRAYTON
1563-1631

Michael Drayton known as 'golden-mouthed Drayton' was a poet friend of Shakespeare's and Ben Jonson. He often went to stay at Clifford Chambers near Shakespeare's home at Stratford, and was present the last time Shakespeare appeared in public. In March 1616 the three had a 'a merry meeting' and it seems they may have over indulged for we learn that Shakespeare 'died of a fever there contracted'.

Both Shakespeare and Drayton were known to the populace for their celebration of King Henry's victories in France: Shakespeare in plays and Drayton in verse. Drayton wasn't head of the class at playwrighting but he was a better sonneteer than his friend whose poems in this form have a little too much rum-tiddly-tum for me.

I don't think anyone has described the break-up between lovers better than Drayton does in his Sonnet 61. None of this stuff — will we or won't we? Stuff the bitterness. Get rid of love as if it's a disease and meet again on equal terms. More power to your man's pen.

SONNET 61

Since there's no help, come let us kiss and part —
Nay, I have done, you get no more of me;
And I am glad, yea, glad with all my heart,
That thus so cleanly I myself can free.
Shake hands for ever, cancel all our vows,
And when we meet at any time again,
Be it not seen in either of our brows
That we one jot of former love retain.
Now at the last gasp of Love's latest breath,
When, his pulse failing, Passion speechless lies,
When Faith is kneeling by his bed of death,
And Innocence is closing up his eyes,
Now, if thou wouldst, when all have given him over,
From death to life thou might'st him yet recover.

EUGENE O'CURRY
1796-1862

6/07/02

It was Eugene O'Curry, a tiny clerk in a lunatic asylum in Clare, who saved a substantial section of ancient Irish literature from perishing. He had resigned in 1833 from the mad house to work for the Ordnance Survey of Ireland. While drawing up boundary lines he also drew stories from the folk around him as well, which he wrote down as the nucleus of a priceless collection of the oldest literature in Western Europe. Had O'Curry not gathered this oral culture it would have perished in the Famine ten years later. O'Curry's collections would be the inspiration of much of the work of Yeats, Synge and Lady Gregory, so he could in a way be termed a founder of the Irish Literary Renaissance. He lost his job in Newman's University on Stephen's Green because of his nationalistic leanings, even though a saintly English cardinal who was dazzled by O'Curry's erudition tried to save him. O'Curry was a poet and his translations from the Irish are not so much translations as new poems. I defy anyone to read the last two lines of 'Do you Remember that Night', the Gaelic version of which he took down in a peasant cabin from the lips of a toothless old woman without feeling some rending of the heart, or perhaps even shedding a tear.

from DO YOU REMEMBER THAT NIGHT

Do you remember that night
When you were at the window,
With neither hat nor gloves
Nor coat to shelter you?
I reached out my hand to you,
And you ardently grasped it;
I remained to converse with you
Until the lark began to sing.

Do you remember that night
That you and I were
At the foot of the rowan-tree,
And the night drifting snow?
Your head on my breast,
And your pipe sweetly playing?
Little thought I that night
That our love ties would loosen!

Beloved of my inmost heart,
Come some night, and soon,
When my people are at rest,
That we may talk together.
My arms shall encircle you
While I relate my sad tale,
That your soft, pleasant converse
Hath deprived me of heaven.

PADRAIC COLUM
1881-1972

13/07/02

In 1967 Padraic Colum, the poet, asked me to the first night of his musical *Carrick na Bauna* featuring Art Carney which opened in New York. As he greeted members of the audience in the foyer some of them said 'It's a pity your father didn't live to see this.'

He had to explain that *he was* the father. The one who had been Yeats' favourite young poet and author of poems like 'The Old Woman of the Road', 'The Drover', 'Cradle Song' and the words of the song 'She Moved Through the Fair'. At eighty-six he looked half his age. He had left Dublin in 1914 for the wrong reason, a pushy wife Molly who wanted to air her learning in New York academic circles. At home he had made his mark in letters, Yeats described him in 1903 as 'a man of genius in the first dark gropings of his mind' and he'd had a hit with his play *The Fiddler's House*, the first realist work at the Abbey Theatre.

But he never improved on these until his wife's death in 1961. He came back after that to Dublin each year and holed up in his sister Susan's house at 11 Edenvale Road, Ranelagh, where I used to visit him for a chuckle and a chat. Here he would recall how at the turn of the century, he and the young Herbert Hughes, the composer, would spend the afternoon together stringing music and phrases together that they had picked up from ballads. Hughes who later had a palatial mansion on Hyde Park corner used to refer to these musical afternoons as 'the slaughter of the symphonies'. It was during one of them that 'She Moved Through the Fair' came into being, which would become the theme song of the film *Michael Collins*. It is an almost perfect piece whose only flaw is the phrase 'Her feet made no din' shoved in to make a rhyme with the word 'in'.

SHE MOVED THROUGH THE FAIR

My young love said to me my mother won't mind,
And my father won't slight you for your lack of kind.
Then she stepped away from me and this she did say,
It will not be long, love, till our wedding day.

Then she stepped away from me and she moved through the fair,
And fondly I watched her move here and move there.
And then she went homeward with one star awake,
As a swan in the evening moves over the lake.

The people were saying no two were e'er wed
But one had a sorrow that never was said,
And I smiled as she passed with her goods and her gear,
And that was the last that I saw of my dear.

Last night she came to me she came softly in,
So softly she came that her feet made no din.
She stepped away from me and this she did say,
It will not be long, love, till our wedding day.

T. W. ROLLESTON
1857-1920

20/02/02

T. W. Rolleston was a prolific enough verse writer but he only wrote one true poem: 'Clonmacnoise' (a translation from the Irish of Angus O'Gillan). This is enough to make you immortal, but the wonder is, as with John Boyle O'Reilly's 'A White Rose', how a man can strike the gong once on a true note and not ever again. Rolleston's poem 'Clonmacnoise' catches the kingly past of our country and the rich monastic culture which preceded it. He was the son of an Offaly judge who went to school at St Columba's, Rathfarnham, and later to Trinity College. Though he was a civil servant in Dublin Castle, he was (like Yeats) a member of the Irish Republican Brotherhood. He went to live in England when he was fifty-one and during the war translated German documents for the Foreign Office. A mysterious man, he died in England in 1920 at a time when the Black and Tans were footloose around Shannonbridge where the mighty monument he wrote about still stands. The last line is, as Leyton Hewitt would say, 'a ripper'.

from CLONMACNOISE

In a quiet water'd land, a land of roses,
Stands Saint Kieran's city fair;
And the warriors of Erin in their famous generations
Slumber there.

There beneath the dewy hillside sleep the noblest
Of the clan of Conn,
Each below his stone with name in branching Ogham
And the sacred knot thereon.

There they laid to rest the seven Kings of Tara,
There the sons of Cairbrè sleep-
Battle-banners of the Gael that in Kieran's plain of crosses
Now their final hosting keep.

Many and many a son of Conn the Hundred-fighter
In the red earth lies at rest;
Many a blue eye of Clan Colman the turf covers,
Many a swan-white breast.

W. B. YEATS
1866-1939

25/05/02

The most famous love sonnet of the twentieth century is undoubtedly Yeats 'When you are old'. It is written to Maud Gonne who was herself a legend in her time. From a Mayo background, but an ascendancy family, she had become such an influential political figure in her twenties that Clemenceau, the evil French prime minister who sewed the seeds at Versailles for the Second World War declared that Maud Gonne had to be broken because of her influence in turning France against England. Throughout his life Yeats remained obsessed with her. No wonder. W. T. Stead, of the London *Times* wrote, after meeting her in Moscow where she was on a secret mission for the French government, 'Maud Gonne is the most beautiful woman in Europe.' She chose, however, her own country to devote all her energies to in freeing it from English rule. When Queen Victoria arrived in 1900 in Dublin she was greeted in O'Connell Street by Maud Gonne and Willie Yeats who were carrying a coffin draped in black. She had an acute social conscience and, among many other achievements for the poor, organised the first warm meal for school children in Dublin in 1912 as well as playing an important part in the reduction of nasal disease in children in the filthy atmosphere of the Dublin slums. With her beauty and intellect she also had a devastating sense of humour. A Great Dane dog, as big as a pony, accompanied her through Dublin who she always introduced with elaborate courtesy to the uneasy Special Branch men of the RIC who shadowed her.

Her legend is still alive among Dublin people. At her son Seán MacBride's funeral (he had won the Nobel Prize for peace and the Lenin Prize for peace), outside the Pro Cathedral an old lady took me by the hand and said 'You could listen to her all night'. There was no doubt as to whom she was referring.

WHEN YOU ARE OLD

When you are old and grey and full of sleep,
And nodding by the fire, take down this book,
And slowly read, and dream of the soft look
Your eyes had once, and of their shadows deep;

How many loved your moments of glad grace,
And loved your beauty with love false or true,
But one man loved the pilgrim soul in you,
And loved the sorrows of your changing face;

And bending down beside the glowing bars,
Murmur, a little sadly, how Love fled
And paced upon the mountains overhead
And hid his face amid a crowd of stars.

JOSEPH PLUNKETT
1887-1916

27/07/02

Joseph Plunkett laid out the military plan for the 1916 rebellion, in between writing poetry, founding a theatre to rival the Abbey, developing the first colour photograph in Ireland and becoming rollerskating champion of Algiers.

His poem 'I See His Blood upon the Rose' is known and revered in the most unexpected places. Once in an audience with the wife of the Emperor of Japan, Princess Michiko, I recited Plunkett's poem to her to show the similarity between the Irish belief of God in nature and the Japanese sense of the divine in their mountains and valleys. Horrifically, half-way through I forgot a line which the Princess with infinite tact supplied for me, revealing that she knew the poem by heart herself, but she was far too well bred to tell me.

Plunkett had been at an English public school, Stonyhurst, and his father and mother who were very rich, employed Edward Carson's father as their architect to build the two beautiful Dublin roads, Palmerston and Marlborough. He has continually been underestimated. Military experts today consider Plunkett's battle-plan for the Rising a strategic masterpiece which would have had considerably more effect if some fool hadn't forgotten to cut the telephone line to Dublin Castle.

I SEE HIS BLOOD UPON THE ROSE

I see his blood upon the rose
And in the stars the glory of his eyes,
His body gleams amid eternal snows,
His tears fall from the skies.

I see his face in every flower;
The thunder and the singing of the birds
Are but his voice — and carven by his power
Rocks are his written words.

All pathways by his feet are worn,
His strong heart stirs the ever-beating sea,
His crown of thorns is twined with every thorn,
His cross is every tree.

ALFRED DOUGLAS
1870-1945

3/08/02

Lord Alfred Douglas was a handsome young rake at Oxford, who after Oscar Wilde had fallen in love with him, got the poet into the most appalling trouble. Douglas had a lot of things going for him. He was three mile champion of Oxford University, a good poet, a master of the sonnet and in social circles was regarded as one of the best looking men in England. His father, the Marquis of Queensberry, had invented the rules of boxing. Alfred Douglas's best poem 'The Dead Poet' is written to the man he ruined, his friend Oscar Wilde. No one has caught the effect of Wilde's magical conversation as Douglas has in the first section of the poem.

After Wilde's death, Douglas lived out his life in a sort of perpetual fury, embroiled in libel actions and bemoaning his lack of recognition as a poet. The climax came when Yeats failed to include any of his work in the *Oxford Book of Modern Verse* (1936) and received a telegram from the indignant author: 'Your omission of my work from the absurdly-named *Oxford Book of Modern Verse* is exactly typical of the attitude of the minor to the major poet, Shoneen Irish would be a more correct name for your book.'

from THE DEAD POET

I dreamed of him last night, I saw his face
All radiant and unshadowed of distress,
And as of old, in music measureless,
I heard his golden voice and marked him trace
Under the common thing the hidden grace,
And conjure wonder out of emptiness,
Till mean things put on beauty like a dress
And all the world was an enchanted place ...

Paris 1901

CHARLES WOLFE
1791-1823

10/08/02

Charles Wolfe is another 'one poem' scribe who hit the target once and never again. He could be top of the class in this category, however, for Lord Byron has referred to Wolfe's 'The Burial of Sir John Moore' as 'the most perfect ode in the language'.

It was through this poem that I had a fifteen seconds of fame on an ITV quiz programme, *Cabbages and Kings*. Members of the panel included Richard Ingrams and Alan Coren, editor of *Punch*, while the quizmaster was Robin Ray, son of Ted Ray the comedian. The question was who was the author of 'The Burial of Sir John Moore' and when Alan Coren said 'William Collins', he was judged correct. Like a shot off a shovel, I was in to say the author was not William Collins but the Reverend Charles Wolfe from County Kildare, a Trinity College Dublin clergyman and a relative of Wolfe Tone. This put the cat among the pigeons of course, but a researcher checked and found I was right. The rest of the panel (with the exception of Ingrams) wanted to re-run this part of the show (which wasn't going out live) but the director (who had the good Mancunian name of Murphy) knew a good piece of television when he saw it and screened the episode warts and all.

from THE BURIAL OF SIR JOHN MOORE AFTER CORUNNA

We buried him darkly at dead of night
The sods with our bayonets turning,
By the struggling moonbeam's misty light
And the lanthorn dimly burning.

No useless coffin enclosed his breast,
Not in sheet or in shroud we wound him;
But he lay like a warrior taking his rest
With his martial cloak around him.

But half of our heavy task was done
When the clock struck the hour for retiring;
And we heard the distant and random gun
That the foe was sullenly firing.

Slowly and sadly we laid him down,
From the field of his fame, fresh and gory;
We carved not a line, and we raised not a stone,
But we left him alone with his glory.

WILLIAM BLAKE
1757-1827

24/08/02

When you listen to a London audience each year at the end of the Proms exulting in 'England's green and pleasant land' it's no harm to remember that these words were written by the son of an Irish tailor, William Blake. It is not of course a hymn to England, but a warning of the destruction that could overtake the country with the coming of the Industrial Revolution. It was Blake who first foresaw the evils of 'the dark satanic mills' which would enslave many millions of workers exploited by the cold hand of capital.

The reference in the first verse is based on a belief that Christ visited England as a young man before embarking on his apostalate in Judea. William Blake's poem has the fiery mysticism of an ancient Irish druid, expressed in the beautiful English of a city only a century or two removed from the singing speech of Shakespeare. Luckily Blake's work found a composer of genius in Hubert Parry to set it to music which is why today it is sung more than any other English piece. It is, by the way, as well a fine anti-globalisation rallying call.

JERUSALEM

And did those feet in ancient time
Walk upon England's mountains green?
And was the holy Lamb of God
On England's pleasant pastures seen?

And did the countenance divine
Shine forth upon our clouded hills?
And was Jerusalem builded here
Among these dark Satanic mills?

Bring me my bow of burning gold!
Bring me my arrows of desire!
Bring me my spear: O clouds, unfold!
Bring me my chariot of fire!

I will not cease from mental fight,
Nor shall my sword sleep in my hand,
Till we have built Jerusalem
In England's green and pleasant land.

ROY CAMPBELL
1901-1957

31/08/02

Roy Campbell was one of the best poets writing in English between the wars. A South African, whose forebears were from Donegal (not Scotland, as is usually thought), he was a master bullfighter and rifle shot, as well as a poet. An Irish descendent though was unlikely to appeal to the somewhat precious likes of Virginia Woolf, Lytton Stracthey and Aldous Huxley of the Bloomsbury set whom Campbell encountered in London. The situation wasn't helped when Virginia Woolf's lover, Vita Sackville West broke off their affair to run off with Campbell's beautiful wife Mary Garmon. However, Mary soon returned to the Campbell nest and they both went off to live happily in Sintra, Portugal, from where I once received a letter from Campbell, showering fire and brimstone on the BBC, whom he unfairly represented as run by 'semites and sodomites'.

Campbell's poem 'The Sisters' catches wonderfully an erotic flavour of colonial Africa. He found the inspiration for it, when as a young eighteen year old he had hidden himself up a tree to shoot bush pigs and in the early morning saw two beautiful girls, (one of whom, Joan Tatham, he was in love with) ride naked on their horses to an inlet at low tide. When I met Roy's nephew, Dr Hamish Campbell, in Durban five years ago, he told me that Joan Tatham's father had threatened to blow the head off a previous admirer of his daughter, so Roy was never quite at ease whenever he would recite this poem in a Durban drawing room.

from THE SISTERS

After hot loveless nights, when cold winds stream
Sprinkling the frost and dew, before the light,
Bored with the foolish things that girls must dream
Because their beds are empty of delight,

Two sisters rise and strip. Out from the night
Their horses run to their low-whistled pleas—
Vast phantom shapes with eyeballs rolling white
That sneeze a fiery steam about their knees.

The frost stings sweetly with a burning kiss
As intimate as love, as cold as death:
Their lips, whereon delicious tremors hiss,
Fume with the ghostly pollen of their breath.

Far out on the grey silence of the flood
They watch the dawn in smouldering gyres expand
Beyond them and the day burns through their blood
Like a white candle through a shuttered hand.

WILLIAM CORY
1823-1892

7/09/02

Many people know the Eton Boating Song with its famous chorus:

>Jolly boating weather,
>And a hay harvest breeze,
>Blade on the feather
>Shade of the trees
>Swing swing together
>With your body between your knees

The author was an Eton English Master, William Cory, who after twenty-six years in the school was reprimanded by headmaster Hornby for interpreting the words a little too heartily in relation to a classical scholar in the upper Sixth, and received orders to depart *instanter*, books and furniture to be collected next day.

Cory was, in his own right, a fine poet who figures in all the major anthologies. A poem he wrote about friendship is one of the most beautiful in the English language, and since it was based on an original Greek version would have brought no repercussions to the author. A phrase from it 'tired the sun with talking' has become part of everyday speech. 'Heraclitus' by Cory also shows how a translation may sometimes exceed the original and become a work of art in itself.

Cory was a resilient bloke and at fifty-five, having gone to live in Madeira, married the good-looking twenty-year-old daughter of a local clergyman who duly bore him a bouncing boy.

HERACLITUS

They told me Heraclitus, they told me you were dead,
They brought me bitter news to hear and bitter tears to shed.
I wept as I remember'd how often you and I
Had tired the sun with talking and sent him down the sky.

And now that thou art lying, my dear old Carian guest,
A handful of grey ashes, long, long ago at rest,
Still are thy pleasant voices, thy nightingales, awake;
For Death, he taketh all away, but them he cannot take.

W. E. HENLEY
1849-1903

14/09/02

William Ernest Henley was an influential critic and editor in London in the 1890s who championed Oscar Wilde and W. B. Yeats. He had only one leg which made him an ideal choice for his friend Robert Louis Stevenson to use him as the model for Long John Silver in *Treasure Island*.

Henley, Judas-like, turned on Oscar Wilde, and after Wilde's arrest on charges of indecency described him as

> An obscene impostor who has transferred his vanities and vices from Trinity College Dublin to London.

Yeats despised this treachery and accused Henley of 'mixing the poison bowl for Wilde'.

Henley wrote several books of indifferent poetry and is credited with being the first to write *vers libre* in English. The extraordinary thing is that this nasty little man should have turned out a splendid poem 'Invictus', whose stirring message can be found in every reputable anthology.

from INVICTUS

Out of the night that covers me,
Black as the pit from pole to pole,
I thank whatever gods may be
For my unconquerable soul.

In the fell clutch of circumstance
I have not winced nor cried aloud.
Under the bludgeonings of chance
My head is bloody, but unbow'd.

Beyond this place of wrath and tears
Looms but the Horror of the shade,
And yet the menace of the years
Finds and shall find me unafraid.

It matters not how strait the gate,
How charged with punishments the scroll,
I am the master of my fate:
I am the captain of my soul.

FRANCIS THOMPSON
1859-1907

21/09/02

Among the drop-outs who used to sleep under London Bridge in the 1880s was an opium addict, Francis Thompson, a former medical student from Lancashire, who was writing a long poem about God's pursuit of man's soul, 'The Hound of Heaven'. Finally, he left it into a publisher, held together with string, but forgot to put his name and address with it. After a year or so the publishers located him and Thompson's fame as a poet was assured.

Curiously, even in the deepest depths of his drug addiction, Francis Thompson never lost his love of cricket, which he had acquired as a schoolboy in Manchester. Borrowing a coat to cover his tramp's clothes he would sneak into Lords cricket ground for the annual match between Lancashire and Yorkshire, known as the War of the Roses, red for Lancashire, white for their opponents. Out of this experience he got one of the most beautiful sports poems in any language. The third last line with its term 'run stealers' (two heroes of the author) catches the image of cricket as if played on a silent film screen before the eye.

from AT LORD'S

It is little I repair to the matches of the Southron folk,
Though my own red roses there may blow;
It is little I repair to the matches of the Southron folk,
Though the red roses crest the caps, I know
For the field is full of shades as I near the shadowy coast,
And a ghostly batsman plays to the bowling of a ghost,
And I look through my tears on a soundless-clapping host
As the run-stealers flicker to and fro,
To and fro:
O my Hornby and my Barlow long ago!

WILLIAM SHAKESPEARE
1564-1616

On this day sixty years ago a mighty armada set out from southern England for the shores of Normandy. They were commanded by an American general who delivered — before they left — a stirring address to the English and American soldiers who comprised the invasion army. No matter how fine a speech he delivered, however, he could never have come within an ass's roar of King Henry V's address to his troops before they set out to conquer France at Agincourt 1415. England won that day and would remain an enemy until the last century when with France as their ally, they fought two wars against Germany. Things changed again just a few months ago when for the first time France and Germany joined together after the British made the decision to sign up with the American carpet baggers who invaded Iraq.

Here is Shakespeare's version in his play *King Henry V* of the famous speech after the 'martial train' had landed at Caux, north of the Seine.

from KING HENRY V

Once more unto the breach, dear friends, once more;
Or close the wall up with our English dead.
In peace there's nothing so becomes a man
As modest stillness and humility:
But when the blast of war blows in our ears,
Then imitate the action of the tiger;
Stiffen the sinews, summon up the blood,
… On, on, you noblest English!
Whose blood has come from fathers of war-proof;
Fathers that, like so many Alexanders,
Have in these parts from morn till even fought,
And sheath'd their swords for lack of argument.
… And you, good yeomen,
Whose limbs were made in England, show us here
The mettle of your pasture; let us swear
That you are worth your breeding; which I doubt not;
For there is none of you so mean and base
That had not noble lustre in your eyes.
I see you stand like greyhounds in the slips,
Straining upon the start. The game's afoot:
Follow your spirit; and upon this charge
Cry 'God for Harry! England and Saint George!'

WILLIAM ALLINGHAM
1824-1889

28/09/02

William Allingham is best remembered for his 'Adieu to Belashanny', an affectionate poem about his native town Ballyshannon, County Donegal. Of minor gentry background, Allingham became a civil servant in London where he gained a reputation as a critic and became a well-known figure in literary circles which included Tennyson, Browning and Rosetti. He was much admired for a long narrative poem, 'Lawrence Bloomfield in Ireland', which is in fact a bore and could suggest that the author was a mere versifier. Yet anyone who reads an extraordinary seven line poem that he wrote one day after a short walk in the countryside could have no doubt that Allingham had the touch which can turn simple words into glistening diamonds. You can read it again and again and it will never cease to move your mind in one way or another.

FOUR DUCKS ON A POND

Four ducks on a pond,
A grass-bank beyond,
A blue sky of spring,
White clouds on the wing;
What a little thing
To remember for years -
To remember with tears!

KATHERINE TYNAN
1861-1931

19/10/02

Katherine Tynan was a teenage poet in the Dublin of the 1890s
with a farmer father who admired his daughter's gifts and ran a
literary salon for her. They lived in Clondalkin and the youthful
Yeats with his friends George Russell and Padraic Colum used
to trek out on Sundays for the fine scoff provided by farmer
Tynan to read their poems to each other. It was thought that
Yeats and Katherine might make an item, but Maud Gonne's
radiant beauty came between them. Katherine who later moved
to London wrote over one hundred novels and three very good
books of memoirs.

Though Yeats admired her poetry he didn't think her quite
good enough for the *Oxford Book of Modern Verse* which he
compiled in 1935. Luckily Katherine had died four years before,
otherwise she probably would have given Willy a good beating
over the head with her umbrella. It was, in a way, unfair of Yeats
to leave her out because he included one or two young hussies
who were making up to him at the time in order to be chosen.

For anyone living in Dublin forty years ago Katherine's
'Sheep and Lambs' will evoke memories of the herds of animals
clattering through the streets making for the golden yellow and
purple hills beyond.

from SHEEP AND LAMBS

All in the April evening,
April airs were abroad;
The sheep with their little lambs
Passed me by on the road.

The sheep with their little lambs
Passed me by on the road;
All in an April evening,
I thought on the Lamb of God.

The lambs were weary, and crying
With a weak, human cry.
I thought on the Lamb of God
Going meekly to die.

Up in the blue, blue mountains
Dewy pastures are sweet;
Rest for the little bodies,
Rest for the little feet.

But for the Lamb of God
Up on the hill-top green,
Only a Cross of shame,
Two stark crosses between...

FREDERICK RODERICK HIGGINS
1896-1941

2/11/02

Fred Higgins sounds more like the name of a snooker player than a poet, but it is the name of one of the finest poets of modern Ireland whose people came from Higginsbrook House in Co Meath. Though Higgins came from an ascendancy background he was an ardent socialist who founded the clerical workers union in the 1930s. He was never well off though and earned his living editing trade magazines before he was made manager of the Abbey by W. B. Yeats who valued his poetry highly.

Like James Stephens, Higgins had an ear for Gaelic poetry and he used its halting rhythm in many of his poems. If you read his 'Father and Son' out loud the carefully stressed beat can come up and the poem will play itself in front of your eyes like a motion picture. The subject is a peculiarly Irish one, that of the close bond between a father and a son which often is not expressed either in words or emotion.

The three lines at the beginning of the second verse which refer to the heron have a special relevance for me. I was reciting them once walking along the river on the Lower Dodder Road with a friend, Gerry O'Flaherty, and as I did a heron flapped out from a tree overhead and flew over a nearby house which I later found out had belonged to F. R. Higgins. I know it sounds a porky, but you can check with Gerry O'Flaherty whom I will put you in touch with if you really feel I'm having you on.

FATHER AND SON

Only last week, walking the hushed fields
Of our most lovely Meath, now thinned by November,
I came to where the road from Laracor leads
To the Boyne river - that seemed more lake than river,
Stretched in uneasy light and stript of reeds.

And walking longside an old weir
Of my people's, where nothing stirs — only the shadowed
Leaden flight of a heron up the lean air —
I went unmanly with grief, knowing how my father,
Happy though captive in years, walked last with me there.

Yes, happy in Meath with me for a day
He walked, taking stock of herds hid in their own breathing;
And naming colts, gusty as wind, once steered by his hand;
Lightnings winked in the eyes that were half shy in greeting
Old friends — the wild blades, when he gallivanted the land.

For that proud, wayward man now my heart breaks —
Breaks for that man whose mind was a secret eyrie,
Whose kind hand was sole signet of his race,
Who curbed me, scorned my green ways, yet increasingly loved me
Till death drew its grey blind down his face.

RUPERT BROOKE
1887-1915

9/11/02

I think the best poem written by any poet about their country is Rupert Brooke's 'The Soldier'. The son of a housemaster at Rugby, a wonderful athlete and rugby player with his golden hair, blue eyes and perfect profile, he typified the ideal Anglo-Saxon type. After Brooke's death in 1915 in the Great War, Winston Churchill tried to exploit him as an icon of the upper class. But actually Brooke was an advanced socialist in the Keynesian mould, one of a group who would go on to create the welfare state in England in 1945. This view was confirmed to me by his closest friend, Geoffrey Keynes, who sent me the collected letters of Brooke which he had edited, and which sets out Brooke's deep dissatisfaction with the social system as it then stood.

Brooke was already recognised as an important poet when at the age of twenty-seven he volunteered for the Royal Naval Division in 1914 when war was declared. In 1915 he was preparing to land at Gallipoli from the flagship of General Sir Ian Hamilton when he contracted blood poisoning which proved fatal. He had just completed six sonnets which Winston Churchill, then First Lord of the Admiralty, saw could be exploited for war propaganda. Churchill got them into *The Times* where they swept the nation, which was in shock after the appalling carnage of the Gallipoli landings. The result was that the establishment converted Brooke into a sort of Nazi hero of the Horst Wessel type, when in fact his political beliefs were quite the opposite. He might in fact have provided a bridge between England and Ireland because he admired James Stephens' *The Crock of Gold* beyond belief and Yeats was one of his heroes. Francis Ledwidge, the Irish soldier poet, who was killed two years later fighting in Salonika, regarded Brooke as a fellow seeker after liberty and commemorated him in verse ('His little England full of lovely noons') along with Thomas McDonagh, Joseph Plunkett and Patrick Pearse.

THE SOLDIER

If I should die, think only this of me:
That there's some corner of a foreign field
That is for ever England. There shall be
In that rich earth a richer dust conceal'd;
A dust whom England bore, shaped, made aware,
Gave, once, her flowers to love, her ways to roam,
A body of England's, breathing English air.
Wash'd by the rivers, blest by suns of home.
And think, this heart, all evil shed away,
A pulse in the eternal mind, no less
Gives somewhere back the thoughts by England given;
Her sights and sounds; dreams happy as her day;
And laughter, learnt of friends; and gentleness,
In hearts at peace, under an English heaven.

ALICE MEYNELL
1847-1922

16/11/02

The poetess Alice Meynell was a real beaut, a Victorian pin-up. It was thought when the Poet Laureateship became available in 1913 that she might be appointed, and one newspaper put Kipling and herself as front runners above Thomas Hardy and Robert Bridges, though in the end John Masefield got the job. She held literary evenings once a week at which her husband Wilfred, the editor of the literary magazine, *Merrie England*, presided and her son and daughter, Everard and Viola, who were both poets, served tea.

She had become a convert to Catholicism on her marriage to Wilfred Meynell. As a Catholic, to have a lover outside marriage would mean committing mortal sin, a serious matter for if you died in that state you could fry forever in the flames. But the bold Alice, having learnt that according to Catholic doctrine for a mortal sin to be committed there must be full and free consent by the person concerned, hit on an ingenious solution. In sleep the faculty of consent is suspended so she would meet her lover only in her dreams. Well, it's one way of having jam on your bread and butter on both sides. Despite, or perhaps because, of this sweet cheat, 'Renouncement' remains one of the great Victorian sonnets, as good a love poem as any her rival Christina Rossetti might have written.

RENOUNCEMENT

I must not think of thee; and, tired yet strong,
I shun the love that lurks in all delight-
The love of thee - and in the blue heaven's height,
And in the dearest passage of a song.

Oh, just beyond the fairest thoughts that throng
This breast, the thought of thee waits hidden yet bright;
But it must never, never come in sight;
I must stop short of thee the whole day long.

But when sleep comes to close each difficult day,
When night gives pause to the long watch I keep,
And all my bonds I needs must loose apart,
Must doff my will as raiment laid away, -
With the first dream that comes with the first sleep
I run, I run, I am gather'd to thy heart.

BRENDAN BEHAN
1923-1964

23/11/02

Next week is the 102nd anniversary of Oscar Wilde's death so let's have a look at a magnificent poem written in tribute to him by fellow Dubliner Brendan Behan. As Brendan insisted on writing all his poetry in the Gaelic I have taken the liberty of using my translation of the poem here. Like Oscar, Brendan was almost as well known in Paris as he was in London. Somehow the torrent of Dublin conversation managed to defy the difficulties of translation, and these two boyos could hold a Parisian audience, as rapt listening to them, as they could do in London and Dublin. In Brendan's case he had acquired his French while working in Paris, whereas Oscar had first lisped the gallic vowels at his mother's knee in Merrion Square. Both of them had a Catholic priest at their deathbed. It was Father Cuthbert OP, later attached to Mount Argus in Harold's Cross, Dublin, who in Paris received the dying Oscar into the Catholic Church. Having indulged himself in this life Oscar may have thought he might like to take out a little fire insurance for the next, and it is this manoeuvre that Behan refers to in the superb last four lines of his poem. And who, but Brendan Behan could have described Oscar as 'The Young Prince of Sin', which in Irish is *Óg Phrionsa na Pheacaigh*.

OSCAR WILDE

After all the wit
In a sudden fit
Of fear, he skipped it.
Stretched in the twilight
That body once lively
Dumb in the darkness
In a cold empty room
Quiet, but for candles
Blazing beside him,
His elegant form
And firm gaze exhausted.
With spiteful concierge
Impatient at waiting
For a foreign waster
Who left without paying
The ten per cent service.
Exiled now from Flore
To sanctity's desert
The young prince of Sin
Broken and withered.
Lust left behind him
Gem without lustre
No Pernod for a stiffner
But cold holy water
The young king of Beauty
Narcissus broken.
But the pure star of Mary
As a gleam on the ocean.

ENVOI
Sweet is the way of the sinner
Sad, death without God's
   praise
My life on you, Oscar boy,
Yourself had it both ways.

Translated from the Irish by
Ulick O'Connor

FRANCIS LEDWIDGE
1891-1917

30/11/02

Anthem for Doomed Youth, published this week, is a collection of poems by poets who fought in the First World War. It includes verse by a road ganger from Co Meath, Francis Ledwidge, who wrote one of the most extraordinary poems in the English language about his university professor friend, Thomas McDonagh, executed in the 1916 Rising.

'To Thomas McDonagh' is a small poem but it uses internal word music, like Palestrina used counterpoint to have his phrases take off and soar to the church ceiling. The old Irish poets used internal rhyme in this way and Ledwidge imitates them here making the third or fourth syllable of a line rhyme with the last one of the previous line, as well as retaining the normal scheme of the four line verse. For instance in the first two lines you will see the last word 'cry' rhyme with the fourth word 'sky' in the next line and so on. This was especially appropriate in a poem dedicated to Thomas McDonagh who had achieved a miracle in poetry with his translation of a Gaelic poem The Yellow Bittern using the same internal rhyme.

Ledwidge who wrote his poem in Salonika while he sat in his tent in the khaki uniform of the British Army must have been keenly aware that his friend had been executed in Dublin by soldiers in the same uniform. It is hard to read the poem without feeling the sadness of our island story welling up. Ledwidge wrote other magnificent pastoral poems such as 'A Twilight in Middle March' and 'June' which can be found in Liam O'Meara's recently collected edition. He makes the rich land of the Royal County immortal with beauty whenever his roving poet's eye settles on something to make his pen take fire. (By the way the 'Dark Cow' in the last verse is a metaphor for Ireland).

THOMAS MCDONAGH

He shall not hear the bittern cry
In the wild sky, where he is lain,
Nor voices of the sweeter birds
Above the wailing of the rain.

Nor shall he know when loud March blows
Thro' slanting snows her fanfare shrill,
Blowing to flame the golden cup
Of many an upset daffodil.

But when the Dark Cow leaves the moor,
And pastures poor with greedy weeds,
Perhaps he'll hear her low at morn
Lifting her horn in pleasant meads.

ERNEST DOWSON
1867-1900

21/12/02

Ernest Dowson used to sit in the corner of the Cheshire Cheese pub in London drinking glass after glass of whiskey murmuring as he did 'This is my first today'. This was in the 1890s in London, a decade when doomed poets and artists died early like Francis Thompson (48), Aubrey Beardsley (26), and Oscar Wilde (44). Willie Yeats thought highly of Dowson as a poet maintaining that his best verse was immortal and would 'outlive famous novels, plays and learned histories'. He acted as a sort of minder for the little Englishman and wasn't upset when telegrams would arrive from France from Dowson asking for help: 'Arrested, sell my watch and send proceeds'.

Dowson was infatuated with the young daughter of an Italian restaurant owner and conferred on her iconic status. Her indifference to his love provided the inspiration for his best poem: 'Cynara'. Perhaps if she'd had responded more generously he might never have written it. Ernest Dowson died in London in 1900 at the age of thirty-three having contributed certain stock phrases to the English language like 'days of wine and roses' and 'gone with the wind'.

from CYNARA

Last night, ah, yesternight, betwixt her lips and mine
There fell thy shadow, Cynara! thy breath was shed
Upon my soul between the kisses and the wine;
And I was desolate and sick of an old passion,
Yes, I was desolate and bow'd my head:
I have been faithful to thee, Cynara! in my fashion.

All night upon mine heart I felt her warm heart beat,
Night-long within mine arms in love and sleep she lay;
Surely the kisses of her bought red mouth were sweet;
But I was desolate and sick of an old passion,
When I awoke and found the dawn was gray:
I have been faithful to thee, Cynara! in my fashion.

I cried for madder music and for stronger wine,
But when the feast is finish'd and the lamps expire,
Then falls thy shadow, Cynara! the night is thine;
And I am desolate and sick of an old passion,
Yea, hungry for the lips of my desire:
I have been faithful to thee, Cynara! in my fashion.

W. B. YEATS
1865-1939

28/12/02

As a ten-year-old, after learning it off by heart, I recited Yeats' poem 'Down by the Salley Gardens' to my nanny who wasn't at all impressed. 'That's only a come-all-ye' she said. She had heard it sung on the streets of her native Cookstown, Co Tyrone as a child. Yeats had taken the ballad, and using a little poetic sellotape here and there, transformed it.

A decade ago, at a Yeats commemoration, at his memorial plot in Stephen's Green, his play *The King's Threshold* was presented and I suggested that it commence with the song, 'The Salley Gardens'. We rehearsed for a few weeks on beautiful summer mornings in David Norris' garden in North Great Georges Street, all round which were massive Georgian mansions, many of them now tenements. Whenever 'The Salley Gardens' was sung, like flowers appearing in spring, people emerged on the tenement balconies or opened their windows to sing along with us the words of the song which they knew so well. It was Yeats' dream fulfilled, to belong to 'the book of the people' from which he thought all real literature came.

DOWN BY THE SALLEY GARDENS

Down by the salley gardens my love and I did meet;
She passed the salley gardens with little snow-white feet.
She bid me take love easy, as the leaves grow on the tree;
But I, being young and foolish, with her would not agree.

In a field by the river my love and I did stand,
And on my leaning shoulder she laid her snow-white hand
She bid me take life easy, as the grass grows on the weirs;
But I was young and foolish, and now am full of tears.

SIR JOHN SQUIRE
1884-1958

3/01/03

A number of writers have been great rugby fans. Louis McNiece, the poet for instance, and Liam O'Flaherty the novelist. But I know only one poem about the game that is worthwhile — Sir John Squire's account of an Oxford and Cambridge match at the Queen's Club before the First World War. Because he had bad sight, Squire found himself exempt from war service, so by the time the ceasefire came in 1918, he had the literary scene in London sewn up. He had become literary editor of *The Observer*, *The New Statesman*, *The Saturday Westminster Gazette* as well as the owner of the *London Mercury* magazine. Younger writers used to grumble about the influence of what they called the Squirearchy. However, eventually Jack Squire, who was a decent cove, found room for them, and as well, he himself occasionally produced a first class poem. He also ran a formidable amateur cricket side, The Invalids, which included Alec Waugh (Evelyn's brother) and Clifford Bax, where he was an invaluable captain but couldn't bat for toffee. Sometime in the 1930s he organised an enormous dinner in honour of himself and some weeks later was knighted for his services to literature. Here's how he saw the end of the Varsity match.

from THE RUGGER MATCH

The ball soars, slackens, keeps upright with effort
Then floats between posts and falls ignored, to the ground,
Its grandeur gone, while the touch-judge flaps his flag,
Nothing can happen now. The attention drifts.
There's a pause; I become a separate thing again,
Almost forget the game, forget my neighbours,
And the noise fades in my ears to a dim rumour.
I watch the lines and colours of field and buildings,
So simple and soft and few in the vapoury air,
I am held by the brightening orange lights of the matches
Perpetually pricking the haze across the ground,
And the scene is tinged with quiet melancholy,
The harmonious sadness of twilight on willowed waters,
Still avenues or harbours seen from the sea.
Sudden one phantom form on the other wing
Emerges from nothingness, is singled out,
Curving in a long sweep like a flying gull.
Through the thick fog, swifter as borne by wind,
Swerves at the place where the corner-flag must be,
And runs, by Heaven he's over! and runs, and runs.

ROBIN FLOWER
1881-1946

11/01/03

Robin Flower was a very decent Yorkshire scholar whose idea of paradise was to live on the Great Blasket island. He had learnt Irish there and found among the people, a culture hundreds of years old which was on the edge of extinction. The islanders loved him and called him *An Bláithín*. He maintained that the Irish speakers on the island had more European culture in their background than people on the mainland or in Britain. One day he heard an old woman lean forward at the fire and say, *'Cá'il an sneachta bhí comh geal anuirig?'* (Where is the snow that was so bright last year?)

Flower sprang up in excitement to tell them that François Villon, the French poet, said the same thing hundreds of years ago in French. 'Where are the snows of yesteryear? (*Où sont les neiges d'antan?*)

'Well,' said one of the men, 'I've always heard that the French were a clever people and I wouldn't put it past them to have said that before we did.'

Robin Flower did other beautiful translations from the old Irish and his 'Pangur Bán' is in many collections of verse. It has the innocence of the time in the eighth century when Ireland, with its monasteries and universities, was the intellectual centre of Europe — the scholar chasing the words of his poem, as his cat chases his mouse. The scholar also had a pet fly who would take the place of a full stop on the page when his master was away having a nap.

from PANGUR BAN

I and Pangur Ban, my cat,
'Tis a like task we are at:
Hunting mice is his delight,
Hunting words I sit all night.

Oftentimes a mouse will stray
In the hero Pangur's way;
Oftentimes my keen thought set
Takes a meaning in its net.

When a mouse darts from its den
O how glad is Pangur then!
O what gladness do I prove
When I solve the doubts I love!

So in peace our tasks we ply,
Pangur Ban, my cat, and I;
In our arts we find our bliss,
I have mine and he has his.

Practice every day has made
Pangur perfect in his trade;
I get wisdom day and night
Turning darkness into light.

GEORGE RUSSELL (Æ)
1867-1935

18/01/03

There is a plaque on 17 Rathgar Avenue in memory of George Russell but hardly any one I have asked knows who he was. Yet Russell was summoned to the White House by Franklin Roosevelt, President of the United States in the 1930s to advise the American government on agricultural matters, having been a key figure in the development of the co-operative movement here. He was also a famous poet. The arrogant Lord Curzon, Viceroy of India, when he was ill, used to cure himself by reading Russell's poems. Russell also wrote *Deirdre*, the first play for the nucleus of an Abbey Theatre Company headed by the Fay brothers and performed in St Teresa's Hall, Clarendon Street (demolished ten years ago with the goodwill of our charming Dublin Corporation). He was so good a painter that a work of his today can sell for €80,000. An incredible all rounder. A decade ago I spoke at the unveiling of a bust of Russell in Merrion Square which is now almost impossible to find as it's hidden by the bushes. At least it hasn't vanished completely like other O'Connell Street Corporation monuments, The Bowl of Light on O'Connell Bridge or the Millenium Clock in the Liffey under it.

This poem, 'Immortality', is a hymn to the power of the spirit, as against the corrupting influence of a consumer society. Right on the dot for the goings on of today's greedy moneybags.

IMMORTALITY

We must pass like smoke or live within the spirit's fire;
For we can no more than smoke unto the flame return
If our thought has changed to dream, our will unto desire,
As smoke we vanish though the fire may burn.

Lights of infinite pity star the grey dusk of our days:
Surely here is soul: with it we have eternal breath:
In the fire of love we live, or pass by many ways,
By unnumbered ways of dream to death.

DYLAN THOMAS
1914-1953

25/01/03

Fifty years ago this year Dylan Thomas got out of his sick bed in the Chelsea Hotel, New York, and went to the Lion's Head bar. He returned a few hours later announcing 'I have had eighteen straight whiskeys, I think that's the record.' Shortly afterwards he was taken to the nearby St Anthony's Hospital where he died. It was in fashion then for artists to drink themselves to death, as Jack Kerouac and Brendan Behan would do within the next decade. They were public performers who fed on the appetite of television and the tabloid press for stories about the famous who misbehaved. Dylan Thomas was blessed with the most beautiful speaking voice for poetry, a mixture of Welsh pulpit oratory and cultured elocution which he learned from his father. His cherubic face, golden voice and public profile gave him infinite opportunity for pulling birds and he out-*jaggered* Mick when he went on his tours of the United States lecturing the blue rinse women in the ladies clubs.

Dylan Thomas and Patrick Kavanagh are the two finest poets in English since World War II. He was the first to transpose words as the Expressionist artists used paint, using adverbs as adjectives and verbs as nouns 'The louder the sun blooms', 'singing light', 'the lilting house'.

Thomas was very close to his father, a Welsh schoolmaster who brought his son up to be a poet and trained his superb speaking voice. Shortly before his father died, Dylan wrote this magnificent poem to him 'Do Not Go Gentle into that Good Night' and sent it to a friend with the remark, 'The only person I can't show it to is of course my father who doesn't know he's dying.'

from DO NOT GO GENTLE INTO THAT GOOD NIGHT

Do not go gentle into that good night,
Old age should burn and rave at close of day;
Rage, rage against the dying of the light.

Though wise men at their end know dark is right,
Because their words had forked no lightning they
Do not go gentle into that good night.

Good men, the last wave by, crying how bright
Their frail deeds might have danced in a green bay,
Rage, rage against the dying of the light.

Wild men who caught and sang the sun in flight,
And learn, too late, they grieved it on its way,
Do not go gentle into that good night.

And you, my father, there on the sad height,
Curse, bless, me now with your fierce tears, I pray
Do not go gentle into that good night.
Rage, rage against the dying of the light.

CHRISTINA GEORGINA ROSSETTI
1830-1894

1/02/03

Christina Rossetti was a natural poet. Everything she wrote had a sparkling singing undertone. But she tied herself in knots with the religious controversies of the Victorian era. Battles almost as fierce as those fought in the Crimea or India were being enacted back home between two sections of the Church of England, High and Low church. Christina was ultra High which meant she was in favour of crucifixes on the altar as well as candles and incense. As she was very beautiful she had many suitors but God help them if they didn't share her views on High church ritual and in the end she never married. She was a kindly soul who founded a home in Highgate where prostitutes could come for refuge. Her brother, the poet Dante Gabriel Rossetti, was one of the founders of the pre-Raphaelite movement. But at her best, Christina had the edge over him and, had she written more, might have made Tennyson look to his laurels.

Her later years were sad for the onset of Graves disease altered her fine looks and she didn't have to worry about the religion of her suitors because sadly they arrived no more. She was modest enough to give the lovely poem here, which is almost perfect, the simple name of 'Song'.

SONG

When I am dead, my dearest,
Sing no sad songs for me;
Plant thou no roses at my head,
Nor shady cypress tree:
Be the green grass above me
With showers and dewdrops wet;
And if thou wilt, remember,
And if thou wilt, forget.

I shall not see the shadows,
I shall not feel the rain;
I shall not hear the nightingale
Sing on, as if in pain;
And dreaming through the twilight
That doth not rise nor set,
Haply I may remember,
And haply may forget.

OLIVER ST JOHN GOGARTY
1878-1957

8/02/03

An immortal poem can arrive simply in a poet's notebook. Oliver St John Gogarty was lying in the grass at the foot of Kilmashogue watching the sun glint off the granite with the blue bay of Dublin below when his daughter, Brenda, aged six, came up with a look of annoyance on her face. She had been playing in the long grass and her shoes had become stained yellow in colour. Her father explained that this was the pollen from the buttercups. By the time he had driven back to his house in Ely Place he had formed the lovely verses opposite.

Gogarty was Ireland's last Renaissance man. A brilliant surgeon, held by many to be the greatest conversationalist in the world after Oscar Wilde, a champion athlete, a senator, he had seventeen poems chosen by Yeats for the *Oxford Book of Modern Verse,* more than any other poet. This didn't stop Gogarty from saying about Yeats when the Nobel prize winner was starting to get above himself: 'Yeats is getting so aristocratic he is evicting imaginary tenants.'

On the other hand Gogarty didn't like Eamon de Valera, whom he described as looking 'like something uncoiled from the Book of Kells'. Gogarty spent his last years in New York, a fabled character in society, but somewhat irritated at his fame as the model for Buck Mulligan, the dashing outrageous character who figures in his former friend James Joyce's book *Ulysses.*

GOLDEN STOCKINGS

Golden Stockings you had on
In the meadow where you ran;
And your little knees together
Bobbed like pippins in the weather,
When the breezes rush and fight
For those dimples of delight,
And they dance from the pursuit,
And the leaf looks like the fruit.

I have many a sight in mind
That would last if I were blind;
Many verses I could write
That would bring me many a sight.
Now I only see but one,
See you running in the sun,
And the gold-dust coming up
From the trampled butter-cup.

W. B. YEATS
1865-1939

15/02/03

This week eighty-five years ago, Lady Gregory's son, Robert, a pilot in the Royal Flying Corps was shot down by an Austrian plane in Northern Italy. Lady Gregory, to whom most of all we owe today's Abbey Theatre, was devastated by the loss of her 'fair haired son, so gentle and affectionate to me all his life'. She got some comfort from her co-Abbey director and friend Yeats, who wrote an elegiac tribute to the dead pilot which is perhaps the best war poem in the English language. Part of its merit is that it avoids the jingoism inherent in most war poems about the dead. Yeats didn't see Robert Gregory as a German-hater, but as a young man who found in the clouds and in the freedom to roam them, a beauty he had not encountered on earth.

Robert Gregory had been a painter and Yeats thought highly of his work. His modern sets for the Abbey Theatre, done in the style of Yeats' hero, Gordon Craig, caused a sensation, and he had begun to paint on canvas in a way that Sickert and Orpen would do two decades later. Robert Gregory was a famous horseman and as a boxer got to the finals of the French middle weight boxing championship. He was exceptionally handsome and my father used to recall batting at the wicket when Robert Gregory was bowling for Co Galway and seeing him running up the pitch, his fair hair streaming in the wind behind him, to unleash a potentially fearful ball which more often than not took the middle stump with it.

Robert Gregory lies today under an Italian sky commemorated by Yeats' famous poem.

AN IRISH AIRMAN FORESEES HIS DEATH

I know that I shall meet my fate
Somewhere among the clouds above;
Those that I fight I do not hate,
Those that I guard I do not love;
My country is Kiltartan Cross,
My countrymen Kiltartan's poor,
No likely end could bring them loss
Or leave them happier than before.
Nor law, nor duty bade me fight,
Nor public men, nor cheering crowds,
A lonely impulse of delight
Drove to this tumult in the clouds;
I balanced all, brought all to mind,
The years to come seems waste of breath,
A waste of breath the years behind
In balance with this life, this death.

WILFRED OWEN
1893-1918

1/03/03

Wilfred Owen had rotten luck. He had served as an officer throughout World War I and written wonderful poems from the trenches. But he wasn't part of the smart set and only had five poems published, when a week before the war ended he was killed. So he never knew the fame his terrifying evocation of the trenches, and the suffering of the soldiers in them, would subsequently have. Some thought he was the best war poet of the lot, Brooke, Grenfell or Sassoon. Yeats for some reason took a scunner against him and left him out of his *Oxford Book of English Verse* which shows that geniuses too can make mistakes in judging others.

Was there ever a better description of the horrors of war, (which young men on both sides may face soon in the Middle East) than in this extract which describes a wounded soldier being borne from the battlefield.

from DULCE ET DECORUM EST PRO PATRIA MORI
'IT IS SWEET AND PROPER TO DIE FOR ONE'S COUNTRY'

If in some smothering dreams you too could pace
Behind the wagon that we flung him in,
And watch the white eyes writhing in his face,
His hanging face, like a devil's sick of sin;
If you could hear, at every jolt, the blood
Come gargling from the froth-corrupted lungs,
Obscene as cancer, bitter as the cud
Of vile, incurable sores on innocent tongues, -
My friend, you would not tell with such high zest
To children ardent for some desperate glory,
The old Lie: Dulce et decorum est
Pro patria mori.

A. E. HOUSMAN
1859-1936

8/03/03

Alfred Housman was a refined Cambridge critic with a tongue like a hatchet which could demolish those he disliked. He once wrote to his publisher telling him to give permission to a woman composer who had set his poems to music: 'But I'd rather you tell her so as I do not want to write letters to a lady whose name is Birdie.'

Surprisingly he wrote the most warm and beautiful poems about Shropshire (the next county to his native Worcestershire) that are among the best-selling poems of the century. His book *The Shropshire Lad* has never been out of print. Housman was homosexual, a fact which he didn't conceal in those days, much more difficult than it would be to do now. He solved his problem by taking his summer hols in Paris where he could have fun galore without having the constabulary tipping him on the shoulder to take him to the jug. Brendan Behan was a great Housman fan and his mother Kathleen had put music to the poem opposite so that the Cambridge aesthete had more of a following in the Dublin pubs than he would have thought. Perhaps he wouldn't have approved though of Kathleen adding, without acknowledgement, an extra verse by Charles Kingsley beginning 'When all the world was young lad', as I would hear her do whenever she would sing on request in a bar.

(If you are wondering why there is no title it's because Housman detested such things).

With rue my heart is laden
For golden friends I had,
For many a rose-lipt maiden
And many a lightfoot lad.

By brooks too broad for leaping
The lightfoot boys are laid;
The rose-lipt girls are sleeping
In fields where roses fade.

WILLIAM WORDSWORTH
1770-1850

15/03/03

For a real countryman the nicest time to walk in the city is the early morning when the streets are silent, seagulls walk on the street and freshness has not yet been fouled. William Wordsworth, the Cumberland poet, found that such a magical moment could be had if he ventured out at sunrise in London. No poem in the English language catches the heartbeat of a city as Wordsworth's one about Westminster Bridge does. The poem's pulse seems to beat in unison with the great metropolis. Shakespeare and Yeats are the two greatest poets in the English language, but Wordsworth could be said to head the next category. His life had much in common with Yeats who was a revolutionary in his early years, as Wordsworth was when he supported the revolution in Paris in 1789. In later years Wordsworth, however, became decidedly anti-French when Napoleon cast a greedy eye on the white cliffs of Dover.

When one thinks of the hell Dublin has become these days, one envies Wordsworth the peace he enjoyed on Westminister Bridge that morning. The first glimmers of light on O'Connell Bridge today are usually hailed by the shrieks of drunken revellers while the prone bodies of comatose teenagers strew the streets around In the meantime taxis, cars and ambulances are conveying the walking wounded of the night to hospital or their lawful beds. Such has our capital become, with its image closer to a Roman vomitorium than that which it once had, that of the seventh city of Christendom.

UPON WESTMINSTER BRIDGE

Earth has not anything to show more fair:
Dull would he be of soul who could pass by
A sight so touching in its majesty:
This City now doth like a garment wear
The beauty of the morning; silent, bare,
Ships, towers, domes, theatres, and temples lie
Open unto the fields, and to the sky;
All bright and glittering in the smokeless air.
Never did sun more beautifully steep
In his first splendour valley, rock, or hill;
Ne'er saw I, never felt, a calm so deep!
The river glideth at his own sweet will:
Dear God! the very houses seem asleep;
And all that mighty heart is lying still!

JAMES STEPHENS
1883-1950

18/05/02

James Stephens, the poet, was under five feet in height which meant he hadn't too much to haul up when he had competed in rope climbing competitions at which he was Irish champion. Going up and down the rope for long periods gave him plenty of time to polish his rhymes.

Incidentally, James Joyce regarded Stephens as a soul mate as they shared the same birthday in the same year and wanted to write the second half of *Finnegans Wake* in collaboration with him. The lettering under the title would be JJ&S as in John Jameson and Sons. There was a pair of them in it.

Ironically, while Joyce was seriously terrified of dogs Jamesy was inordinately fond of them and used to introduce himself as an 'honorary dog'. I used recite his poem 'The Snare' when I spoke to ladies clubs in the United States and I never failed to notice when I'd finished, a number of eyes blinking a little to shake the moisture from the eyelashes.

from THE SNARE

I hear a sudden cry of pain!
There is a rabbit in a snare:
Now I hear the cry again,
But I cannot tell from where.

But I cannot tell from where
He is calling out for aid!
Crying on the frightened air,
Making everything afraid!

Making everything afraid!
Wrinkling up his little face!
As he cries again for aid;
– And I cannot find the place!

And I cannot find the place
where his paw is in the snare!
Little One! Oh, Little One!
I am searching everywhere!

LEWIS CARROLL
1832-1898

12/04/03

As a kid I was bored with Lewis Carroll's *Alice in Wonderland*. I took the White Rabbit and the March Hare seriously and didn't recognise the surrealistic humour that inspired them. Then I always felt sorry for the poor Dormouse when they stuffed him in the teapot at their party. I think you have to be grown-up to be able to really appreciate Lewis Carroll's wonderful book and relish its fantastic fun. I've always suspected children who claim to be *Alice in Wonderland* fans.

Lewis Carroll was a clergyman and a mathematical genius when he was professor at Oxford. His great friend was Alice Liddell, the nine-year-old daughter of the Dean of his college, and he took hundreds of photographs of her, in the course of which he made technical advances that are still recognised in photography. Alice's adventures influenced our own James Joyce, whose *Finnegans Wake* comes straight out of Humpty Dumpty's pronouncement: 'You see it's like a portmanteau, there are two meanings packed up into one word. But I always pay it extra. Impenetrability, that's what I say.'

The piece that really won me over to Lewis Carroll was *You are old Father Willam*, which is an absolute howl. Don't worry if it doesn't click the first time. Keep at it till you catch the tune.

from YOU ARE OLD FATHER WILLIAM

'You are old, Father William,' the young man said
'And your hair has become very white;
And yet you incessantly stand on your head -
Do you think, at your age, it is right?'

'In my youth', Father William replied to his son,
'I feared it might injure the brain;
But, now that I'm perfectly sure I have none,
Why, I do it again and again.'

 'You are old' said the youth 'and your jaws are too weak
For anything tougher than suet;
Yet you finished the goose, with the bones and the beak -
Pray, how did you manage to do it?'

'In my youth' said his father, 'I took to the law,
And argued each case with my wife;
And the muscular strength, which it gave to my jaw
Has lasted the rest of my life.'

'I have answered three questions, and that is enough'
Said his father, 'Don't give yourself airs!
Do you think I can listen all day to such stuff?
Be off, or I'll kick you downstairs!'

PATRICK PEARSE
1879-1916

19/04/03

Apart from leading a revolution along with James Connolly, Patrick Pearse was a fine poet. 'The Fool' ('Since the wise men have not spoken I speak that I'm only a fool') and 'The Wayfarer' are in many anthologies. But it is a poem written to his mother eighty-seven years ago, in the wake of Easter Week, the night before he and his brother were executed that most appeals to me. Though Pearse was devoted to his mother, it was his father who had the greatest influence on him. James Pearse was a Devonshire sculptor who had come to Ireland as a result of a scheme initiated by William Morris, the English socialist poet, to exchange artists and craftsmen between the two countries. James had written a book, *England's duty to Ireland as it appears to an Englishman,* and contributed frequently to the newspapers on the theme that England 'has no moral right to rule this country'. Patrick used to say affectionately about his father *'Ní raibh sé rómh h-olc mar Shasanach'* (he was not too bad for an Englishman).

Patrick Pearse's ruling passion was teaching and he founded a school, St Enda's, Rathfarnham, where he could put his ideas into practice. He welcomed the Home Rule Bill in 1912 because it would give Ireland control of education. Five years ago, writing in the London *Times*, Lord Rees-Mogg a former editor, remarkably concluded that Patrick Pearse's ideas on teaching were 'a hundred years before his time'. But German guns in Ulster hands stalled the creation of an Irish parliament and Pearse found himself instead in the Post Office in 1916 along with General James Connolly a man, like him, driven by hatred of opression and social injustice.

THE MOTHER

I do not grudge them: Lord, I do not grudge
My two strong sons that I have seen go out
To break their strength and die, they and a few,
In bloody protest for a glorious thing,
They shall be spoken of among their people,
The generations shall remember them,
And call them blessed;
But I will speak their names to my own heart
In the long nights;
The little names that were familiar once
Round my dead hearth.
Lord, thou art hard on mothers:
We suffer in their coming and their going;
And tho' I grudge them not, I weary, weary
Of the long sorrow - And yet I have my joy:
My sons were faithful, and they fought.

CHARLES BAUDELAIRE
1821-1867

26/04/03

It was a delight to find that Charles Baudelaire, the greatest poet of the nineteenth century in English and French cherished the little old ladies whom he would see on the Paris streets. Their courage and determination in accepting the chains of age charmed him and he frequently followed them in the streets to observe them on their daily walks.

The little oul' ones in Dublin were part of the scene years ago and one could see the characteristics in them of wit, dignity and wisdom that Baudelaire had noted in their Paris counterparts. In Dublin they had a special place in the pub reserved for them, the snug where no one could enter without permission. With their families reared they now drank fastidiously only brandy or port. One was always flattered if they asked you to join them.

When Baudelaire's greatest collection of poems, *The Flowers of Evil* (*Les Fleurs du Mal*), was banned by the French courts in 1864 he risked jail rather than change a word. It is touching to think that his poet's eye had perceived, beneath the fragile frame of the old ladies, the same courage that had driven him to write as he did.

LITTLE OLD LADIES

Little old ladies, how often have I followed them!
Especially one who, as the dying sun departs
And vermilion wounds bloody the evening's rim,
Would sit on a park bench, pensive and apart,

Delighting in those concerts with their ringing brass
With which the army sometimes grace our parks,
Making us feel reborn as the golden evenings pass
And some heroism pours into people's hearts.

Her, I recall still, proud, with a queen's stance,
Absorbed in the valour of some martial quarrel.
Sometimes her eye would open with an eagle glance,
The marble forehead lifted for the laurel.

Translated by Ulick O'Connor

L. A. G. STRONG
1896-1958

10/05/03

Few bathing places in the world have the literary credentials of the Forty Foot in Sandycove. George Bernard Shaw and Samuel Beckett swam there, and Joyce opens his novel *Ulysses* in the Martello Tower with his hero Stephan Dedalus looking down on the swimmers in the bathing pool just below him. His friend, Oliver St John Gogarty, poet and champion swimmer (who had two awards for rescuing people from drowning), had hired the Tower so that Joyce could write his novel in which he would celebrate the 'snot-green sea' which greeted him each morning as he descended the iron steps of the Tower. Another avid forty-footer was L. A. G. Strong who has two poems in the *Oxford Book of Modern Verse* as well as having won the James Tate Black memorial prize for his collection of short stories, *Travellers*, in 1945. His charming poem about the place is not well-known though it contains the names of many who were part of Dublin life at the time. By the way, Hy-Brazil referred to in the third line from the end, is a Celtic paradise beyond the sea's edge where the brave are said to reside after death.

THE FORTY-FOOT

Dockrell, Tallon, Beckett then
Were the days of mighty men!
Holmes, McGuinness, Fawcett, Chute
An Eldorado of the brute
Strength and grace of naked man:
Sure, I am that no one can
Swim and dive the like of them.

Dockrell, Tallon, Beckett where
Are the men I worshipped there?
Some still rub the pink flesh dry
Some have laid their towels by
Some go round the round tower still
Some are passed to Hy-Brazil
Where Fawcett, he that dived and died,
Plunges in a fairer tide.

AUSTIN CLARKE
1896-1974

22/03/03

Dispatched by an English publisher as a young man to interview the poet Yeats, Austin Clarke made a fatal mistake. He asked W. B. had he slept with Maud Gonne or not. Yeats' answer was to lead Austin from the room in silence and show him the front door. At the time Austin was in danger of suffocating under the Deirdre-Weirdre school, a false follow-on from the literary renaissance, and this row with Yeats may have done him good.

Born and reared near the Black Church (St Mary's Chapel of Ease, Mountjoy Sreet) he allowed the savage sarcasm of his native city to inspire him, and in the manner of Swift, rather than Yeats, surgically sliced open the hypocritical skin of contemporary Ireland. The new departure began with his book *Flight to Africa* which, as Dylan Thomas was then doing, used all sorts of new arrangements of words and rhymes to get results.

I stray from American, German, tourists,
Greek guide, feel in my two wrists

Austin Clarke's work is a bridge between old and new Ireland as we can see when he praises our new airline Aer Lingus in 'Over Wales'.

OVER WALES

Our aeroplanes fly quicker now. They go
To nineteen thousand feet or more; below,
The whiteness of cloud, cloudlet, unseen.
The upper world seems motionless: machine
Is poised in noise. Pearl, vert, blue, paler hues,
Horizoning. Passengers read the news: ..... One day
Propelled beyond the map of Morcombe Bay,
Outside a hundred miles of hurricane,
I stared at the darkening rollers of thunder-plain,
Flawing, up-snowing, heard the engines thrum
Like hail on the wings of aluminium,
Then, of a sudden, far across the unsaily
Wave-tops, I saw the twinkle of the Baily.
The Airport measured gale force, grounded all flights,
And Ireland came up with its fairy lights.

JOHN DONNE
1573-1631

24/05/03

John Donne, a contemporary of Shakespeare and Ben Johnson, is the only poet to have written a poem on a flea to his lover -

   It's sucked me first and sucks thee
   And in this flea our two bloods mingled be

This is hectic for a chap from a Catholic family who became the Protestant Dean of St Paul's. Down the road from St Paul's was Shakespeare's Globe Theatre where the Stratford upstart was presenting on an open stage the greatest plays ever written. But when it came to writing sonnets the Reverend John Donne puts Shakespeare in the ha'penny place. The last two lines in the sonnet below are among the finest in the English language with their defiant trumpet blast against decay.

DEATH

DEATH, be not proud, though some have called thee
Mighty and dreadful, for thou art not so:
For those whom thou think'st thou dost overthrow
Die not, poor Death; nor yet canst thou kill me.
From Rest and Sleep, which but thy picture be,
Much pleasure, then from thee much more must flow;
And soonest our best men with thee do go -
Rest of their bones and souls' delivery!
Thou'rt slave to fate, chance, kings, and desperate men,
And dost with poison, war, and sickness dwell;
And poppy or charms can make us sleep as well
And better than thy stroke. Why swell'st thou then?
One short sleep past, we wake eternally,
And Death shall be no more: Death, thou shalt die!

PERCY FRENCH
1854-1920

14/06/03

Percy French, from a Roscommon landed gentry family, was one of the leading entertainers of the first half of the twentieth century. His songs and poems were sung and recited throughout England and America. He never got the respect due to him as an artist because he didn't write musicals like Dion Boucicault or Abbey-style poetic dramas and comedies. Songs like 'Phil the Fluters Ball', 'Come back Paddy Reilly to Ballyjamesduff', 'The Mountains of Mourne', 'Slattery's Mounted Foot' remain at the top of the best Irish songs of the century. Percy French accompanied himself on the banjo at which he was an expert. In between songs Percy French used to do remarkable impersonations as well as lightening sketches on the stage which, when they were placed upside down, would turn out to be something else. He was an important landscape painter. A good Percy French could fetch up to €40,000 today, though twenty years ago you could buy them for a tenner. A darling man.

Here's an extract from a fun poem he wrote about Queen Victoria's visit to Dublin in 1900 and how she was greeted by the beautiful rebel Maud Gonne along with her admirer the poet Yeats carrying a black coffin up O'Connell Street.

from THE QUEEN'S AFTER-DINNER SPEECH

(As Overheard and Cut into Lengths of Poetry by Jamesy
Murphy, Deputy-Assistant-Waiter at the Viceregal Lodge)

'And that other wan,' sez she,
'That Maud Gonne' sez she,
'Dhressin' in black,' sez she,
'To welcome me back', sez she;
'Though I don't care,' sez she,
'What they wear,' sez she,
'An' all that gammon,' sez she,
'About me bringin' famine,' sez she,
'Now Maud 'ill write,' sez she,
'That I brought the blight,' sez she,
'Or altered the saysons,' sez she,
'For some private raysins,' sez she,
'An' I think there's a slate,' sez she
'Off Willie Yeats' sez she.
'He should be at home,' sez she,
'French polishin' a pome,' sez she
'An' not writin' letters,' sez she,
'About his betters,' sez she,
'Paradin' me crimes,' sez she,
'In the 'Irish Times',' sez she.
'But what they can't draw,' sez she,
'Is the Lion's claw,' sez she,
'And before our flag's furled,' sez she,
'We'll own the wurruld,' says she.

J. O. WALLIN
1779-1839

28/06/03

Dublin (originally Dyfflin), Cork and Limerick were founded by Vikings. In no other region but Scandanavia will you see as many people with the Irish combination of green eyes and red hair. I came across an eighteenth-century poem by a Swedish archbishop which could have been written by a ninth century monk in his cell in the way it deals with the union of God and nature. I translated it into English and it was sung by the choir, under Isabel McCarthy, at St Nicholas Church of Ireland in Dundalk in a service conducted by that splendid man, the late Archbishop George Simms. Well here it is. Is there not a whiff somewhere in it of St Kevin and his singing birds of Glendalough?

WHERE IS THE FRIEND

Where is the Friend that everywhere I'm seeking?
When daylight comes my longing grows for Thee, King.
When day departs I have not found my Master,
Though the heart beats faster.

I hear his Voice where summer winds are breathing,
Where forests sing, and where the river's seething.
Its splendour fills me, and where that Voice is,
My heart rejoices.

I sense his Being in every move of nature,
The flower that blooms, and bends towards its Creator,
The very air I breathe, each sigh I utter,
Mingles with my Lover.

Be strong my soul, hope, pray, surrender.
Your friend beckons: soon you'll taste how tender
His love can be; and sink upon his Bosom
And never lose Him.

Translated by Ulick O'Connor

LADY GREGORY
1875-1931

5/07/03

Next year is the hundredth anniversary of the founding of the Abbey Theatre. Lady Augusta Gregory was the leading figure in starting the Abbey and keeping it in existence till the State made available enough money to survive in the late 1920s. Not only had she had a flair for the arts, but she had a business instinct that would have made a fortune for her on the stock market today. She collected money for her beloved Abbey in America on numerous tours and saved every penny in Ireland by travelling third class on the railways to add to the fund. She wrote over forty plays, one of which is a masterpiece, *The Workhouse Ward,* and, having learnt Irish, collected hundreds of important folk tales from the people around her in Gort. She had real grit. Once outside the Abbey, as she emerged, the Black and Tans, who were terrorising the city, let a volley of shots fly over her head. Lennox Robinson, who was with her, fled into the theatre but Lady Gregory shook her umbrella at the soldiers and said with her famous lisp: 'Up the webels.'

Why, when they were thinking of defiling the city landscape with that glorified hypodermic needle in O'Connell Street, they didn't think of a statue instead for the Old Lady of nearby Abbey Street. Here's an excerpt from one of her translations of the beautiful Irish song, Donal Óg. It is called 'The Grief of a Girl's Heart'.

from THE GRIEF OF A GIRL'S HEART

O Donal Óg if you cross the sea bring myself with you and do
    not forget it.
And you will have sweetheart for fair days and market days.
And the daughter of the King of Greece beside you at night.

You promised and you said a lie to me
That you would be before me where the sheep are flocked.
I gave a whistle and three hundred cries to you
And I found nothing there but a bleating lamb.

It was on that Sunday I gave my love to you.
The Sunday that was last before Easter.
And myself on my knees reading the Passion.
And my two eyes giving love to you forever.

You have taken the east from me you have taken the west from
    me
You have taken what is before me and what is behind me
You have taken the moon you have taken the sun from me
And my fear is great that you have taken God from me.

THOMAS MOORE
1780-1852

26/07/03

When Robert Emmet, the executed patriot, the anniversary of whose death takes place this year, was a student at Trinity his best friend was a fellow student, Thomas Moore, the poet. Moore knew the beautiful Sarah Curran, daughter of the leading Irish barrister, John Philpot Curran. After Emmet's execution Sarah was heartbroken. A few years later she married a Captain Sturgeon, an engineer in the Royal Staff Corps and nephew of a former English Prime Minister who took her to Sicily to regain her health. But Sarah never really recovered and she died in 1808 at Hythe in Kent, England. She was a lovely girl with a beautiful singing voice and a devotee of Mozart.

It is about Sarah that Tom Moore would write one of his best known poems, which was set to music and sung throughout the world. It is ironic that Moore who had become the darling of the English drawing rooms would also write many beautiful songs about his own country, which would have a powerful impact on the emergence of the national spirit in the nineteenth century.

from SHE IS FAR FROM THE LAND

She is far from the land where her young hero sleeps,
And lovers are round her sighing;
And coldly she turns from their gaze, and weeps,
For her heart in his grave is lying!

She sings the wild songs of her dear native plains,
Every note which he loved awaking:
Ah! little they think who delight in her strains,
How the heart of the minstrel is breaking!

He had lived for his love, for his country he died,
They were all that to life had entwined him;
Nor soon shall the tears of his country be dried,
Nor long will his love stay behind him.

W. B. YEATS
1865-1939

9/08/03

The present uncertainty about the future of Lissadell House is intolerable. The tale of the two sisters who lived there is part of the literary and historical history of Western Europe. The house where James Joyce's family lived was bulldozed recently in Richmond Avenue. Lady Gregory's European famous mansion at Coole, Galway, is now a grass plot. Certain cretins in the Corporation may decide these matters, but worse still are the citizens who accept these decisions with the silence of the lambs. Lissadell simply can't have its character changed. It is inhabited by history and perpetuated in a powerful poem which is known in every civilised country in Western Europe. The poem is dedicated to two sisters Constance and Eva Gore-Booth whose presence still permeates the mansion. As Commandant Markievicz (in the rising she had married a Polish Count), Constance was condemned to death in 1916, and Eva campaigned for many years in Manchester where she joined the socialist movement and devoted her life to working class ideals there. Constance was reprieved and would become the first woman elected to Westminster. That Constance's memory is still alive in the minds of the people I realised many years ago in the old Piper's Club in Thomas Street, when a very old lady got up and after explaining that her 'tubes' were bad; shuffled away in a minimal manner that somehow managed to suggest a dance. 'I was taught be the Countess,' she explained; and for a moment a presence filled the room.

Some think this is Yeats' finest poem.

IN MEMORY OF EVA GORE-BOOTH
AND CON MARKIEWICZ

The light of evening, Lissadell,
Great windows open to the south,
Two girls in silk kimonos, both
Beautiful, one a gazelle.
But a raving autumn shears
Blossom from the summer's wreath;
The older is condemned to death,
Pardoned, drags out lonely years
Conspiring among the ignorant.
I know not what the younger dreams —
Some vague Utopia — and she seems,
When withered old and skeleton-gaunt,
An image of such politics.
Many a time I think to seek
One or the other out and speak
Of that old Georgian mansion, mix
Pictures of the mind, recall
That table and the talk of youth,
Two girls in silk kimonos, both
Beautiful, one a gazelle.
Dear shadows, now you know it all,
All the folly of a fight
With a common wrong or right.
The innocent and the beautiful
Have no enemy but time;
Arise and bid me strike a match
And strike another till time catch;
Should the conflagration climb,
Run till all the sages know.
We the great gazebo built,
They convicted us of guilt;
Bid me strike a match and blow.

HILAIRE BELLOC
1870-1953

30/08/03

Globalisation didn't begin yesterday. Just as cities and towns in Ireland are being ravaged by ugly development today, in the nineteenth century much of Old England was destroyed by the industrial revolution. Hilaire Belloc, the English poet, set out to oppose the destruction of the countryside at the beginning of the twentieth century. In his poem 'Ha'nacker Mill' he embodies the soul of England in a girl's name Sally, who worked in a water-powered mill. The poem deplores the rash of coal powered factories that were to contaminate the beautiful English landscape, what William Blake named 'the dark satanic mills'. There is a lesson for us in Belloc's 'Ha'nacker Mill' with its picture of a desolate countryside with unploughed fields and none to plough them.

Monsignor Ronald Knox used to say about Belloc that 'The undercurrents of his mind were sad and his face never looked happy in repose.' Yet he was in one sense a happy man who faced up to the evils of his age and fought the good fight against them.

HA'NACKER MILL

Sally is gone that was so kindly
Sally is gone from Ha'nacker Hill.
And the Briar grows ever since then so blindly
And ever since then the clapper is still,
And the flaps have fallen from Ha'nacker Mill.

Ha'nacker Hill is in Desolation:
Ruin a-top and a field unploughed,
And spirits that call on a fallen nation
Spirits that loved her calling aloud:
Spirits abroad in a windy cloud.

Spirits that call and no one answers;
Ha'nacker's down and England's done
Wind and Thistle for pipe and dancers
And never a ploughman under the Sun.
Never a ploughman. Never a one.

WILFRED BLUNT
1840-1922

6/09/03

Wilfred Blunt had a red-blooded love of England and could write of the thrill he experienced when he saw 'the red coats marching from the hill' as he sailed into Gibraltar. But he loved justice even more. A rich Sussex land owner, he denounced English atrocities in India in 1905 and the hanging of Roger Casement in 1916. He came to Ireland in 1886 to campaign for the Land League and ended up with a stiff sentence in Galway Jail for a seditious speech against the British government. On his release, he gave his friend Lady Gregory, whom he'd met campaigning for the release of an Egyptian patriot, a piece of tarred rope from the prison which she would use as a bookmark for the rest of her life. It was to remind her of Blunt with whom she'd had an affair when she was in Cairo with her husband Sir William Gregory. Indeed it might be said Blunt played a part in the creation of the Abbey Theatre, because it was he who first encouraged Lady Gregory to write, and brought her into contact with Irish nationalism. He came from one of the old English Catholic families who had never taken a title because they wouldn't change their religion at the Reformation.

Wilfred Blunt was an important poet and is recognised as one of the best writers of the sonnet in the language. 'St Valentine's Day' is a love letter which evokes the English countryside in a way that can make you catch your breath.

ST VALENTINE'S DAY

Today, all day, I rode upon the down,
With hounds and horsemen, a brave company.
On this side in its glory lay the sea,
On that the Sussex weald, a sea of brown.
The wind was light, and brightly the sun shone,
And still we galloped on from gorse to gorse.
And once, when checked, a thrush sang, and my horse
Pricked his quick ears as to a sound unknown.
I knew the Spring was come - I knew it even
Better than all by this, that through my chase
In bush and stone and hill and sea and heaven
I seemed to see and follow still your face.
Your face my quarry was. For it I rode,
My horse a thing of wings, myself a god.

A. E. HOUSMAN
1859-1936

18/10/03

One of the best read poets of all time is A. E. Housman. Though
he was professor of classics at Cambridge he hated academics and
critics whom he accused of 'nursing self complacent airs and who
pass from self complacency to insolence'.

Housman himself didn't quite know how he wrote his
marvellous poetry. Sometimes it came to him ready made on his
tongue, and other times in between college classes he would
pursue rhythms and images for months of rewriting before
getting a few lines down. What saddened him most was the First
World War and the awful slaughter which lost England over two
million of its young men. Some of them were his friends, and it
must of been from one of these he heard how a German enemy,
jumping into a trench to kill the occupants, became a phantom
in the mind of the English soldier who had killed him.

I did not lose my heart in summer's even,
When roses to the moonrise burst apart:
When plumes were under heel and lead was flying,
In blood and smoke and flame I lost my heart.

I lost it to a soldier and a foeman,
A chap that did not kill me, but he tried;
That took the sabre straight and took it striking
And laughed and kissed his hand to me and died.

D. H. LAWRENCE
1885-1930

1/11/03

Mention the book *Lady Chatterley's Lover* by D. H. Lawrence
and watch the eyeballs roll in horror as your listener recalls the
Obscenity trial that greeted the book's publication after
Lawrence's death in 1961, almost in Beatles-time. David
Lawrence was a miner's son from Nottinghamshire who like
Joyce wrote about sex as part of human nature, and ranks next
to him as the best novelist in English of the twentieth century.
Unlike our Jim, however, Lawrence was a genuine mystic who
believed that sexual attraction was part of the Divine plan —
and get on with it.

As well as his famous novels, Lawrence left behind a
Collected Poems as big as the bible. Why haven't we heard more
about these? Simply because taste today is largely determined by
joyless critics and mean academics who are blind to true poetry
and dismiss D. H. Lawrence as a sex maniac. Far from it, as this
extract from his poem 'Shadows' shows, which could have been
approved by Blessed Matt Talbot.

from SHADOWS

And if to-night my soul may find her peace
in sleep, and sink in good oblivion,
and in the morning wake like a new-opened flower
then I have been dipped again in God, and new-created.

then I shall know that my life is moving still
with the dark earth, and drenched
with the deep oblivion of earth's lapse and renewal

then I must know that still
I am in the hands of the unknown God,
he is breaking me down to his own oblivion
to send me forth on a new morning, a new man.

EMILY LAWLESS
1845-1913

15/11/03

The Honourable Emily Lawless, daughter of Lord Cloncurry
was a born rebel. She had a lots of clout to pursue her causes
because everyone read her novels, which were much admired by
Mr Gladstone, the English prime minister. Emily was also a
famous swimmer and diver in her day, who worked off her anger
against those who attacked her by diving naked into the Atlantic
off the massive cliffs of Clare. But it is by her poetry that one
remembers her today and two of her poems are found in every
Irish anthology. These are 'After Aughrim' and 'The Clare
Coast' both of which deal with the Wild Geese, those Irish
gentleman soldiers who, rather than serve under the hated King
Billy, went into exile and served in the Russian, French and
Austrian armies. One Peter Lally from Limerick became
commander-in-chief of the Russian army under Catherine the
Great, another Ulick Browne of Kildare was in charge of the
Empress Marie Therese's army in Austria while a Dillon from
Co Clare was a marshal in the French army, under Louis XIV.
Here are verses from Emily Lawless's 'After Aughrim' in which
the 'She' is Ireland lamenting her lost sons.

from AFTER AUGHRIM

She said, 'They gave me of their best,
They lived, they gave their lives for me;
I tossed them to the howling waste,
And flung them to the foaming sea'.

She said ' I never gave them aught,
Not mine the power, if mine the will;
I let them starve, I let them bleed, -
They bled and starved, and loved me still.'

She said 'I never called them sons,
I almost ceased to breathe their name
They caught it echoing down the wind,
Blown backwards from the lips of Fame.'

She said 'God knows they owe me nought,
I tossed them to the foaming sea,
I tossed them to the howling waste,
Yet still their love comes home to me.'

GERARD MANLEY HOPKINS
1844-1889

22/11/03

In Glasnevin cemetery there is a massive stone tablet that has carved on it in alphabetical order the names of members of the Jesuit community who have died in Ireland.

At the letter H you will find the name Gerard Manley Hopkins, who in my view, is the third best poet in the English language after Shakespeare and Yeats. Hopkins was English and lectured in Greek at the Catholic University, 86 St Stephen's Green. He was a Jesuit who converted from Protestantism and who was to change the face of poetry in the twentieth century. The extraordinary thing is that his verse was never published in his lifetime, except in a few private magazines. At forty-six this lonely genius died of typhoid in a small room overlooking Stephen's Green.

His life was incredibly sad, exiled in a land he only partly understood and no one to hail his genius. Even his friend, the Poet Laureate, Robert Bridges, failed to recognise where Hopkins was at. Like Picasso in painting and Stravinsky in music, he saw the world at an angle different to anything that had gone before and the tilt he gave to reality reveals a new landscape to the reader which was not immediately recognised.

In this poem, 'God's Grandeur', you should speak the poem out to bring up the stressed beat. 'Shook foil' in the second line is the gold foil we see at Christmas gatherings with its forked flash like sheet lightning. His use of the word 'bent', a clapped out one if there ever was, in the second last line is a triumphant evocation of the brooding presence of the Creator.

134

GOD'S GRANDEUR

The world is charged with the grandeur of God.
It will flame out, like shining from shook foil,
It gathers to a greatness, like the ooze of oil
Crushed. Why do men then now reck his rod?
Generations have trod, have trod, have trod;
And all is seared with trade; bleared, smeared with toil;
And wears man's smudge and shares man's smell: the soul
Is bare now, nor can foot feel, being shod.

And for all this, nature is never spent;
There lives the dearest freshness deep down things;
And though the last lights off the black West went
Oh, morning, at the brown brink eastward, springs —
Because the Holy Ghost over the bent
World broods with warm breast and with ah! Bright wings.

R. N. D. WILSON
1899-1953

6/12/03

Oscar Wilde has described the cynic as someone who knows the price of everything and the value of nothing. Robin Wilson, a forgotten Irish poet of the 1930s has put such gentry where they belong in a beautiful little poem in which he sees a swallow panting on the ground after defying the wind, as an example of how we should accept life. He is daring himself, when he rhymes brilliantly at the start of the poem 'most of all' with 'cynical', an impressive verbal coup. George Russell (Æ) praised Wilson's poetry for 'its colour and melody which please eye and ear' and in the aftermath of Yeats calling for a neo-Catholic school in line with certain contemporary French poets, Wilson converted from the Church of Ireland to take up the challenge. Sadly he wasn't to have much time in his new role as he died in his early fifties.

ENEMIES

... And you, O most of all
I hate, whose wisdom is
But to be cynical, -
The knave's analysis.
You who have never known
The heart set wild with a word,
Or seen the swallows blown
Northward when spring has stirred
The wing's rebellion.

I wonder if you found,
Beaten with wind and sun,
A swallow on the ground,
Would even a moment's thought
Trouble you with a fleet
Pain, that such daring brought
Such passionate defeat.

WILLIAM SHAKESPEARE
1564-1616

27/12/03

Had Shakespeare an Irish connection? Certainly his character Captain MacMorris, the Irish soldier in *Henry V*, uses Gaelic phrases that show an acquaintance with our ancient tongue. When Shakespeare takes a fantasy trip in plays like *A Midsummer Nights Dream* and *The Tempest,* at times he could be W. B. Yeats chasing a rainbow. As a Catholic in Stratford, Shakespeare would undoubtedly have met outlawed Irish priests on the run from the King's cavalry. But the great English poet-critic Matthew Arnold thought the Celtic connection in Shakespeare ran deeper than that and maintained that lines in the plays 'are drenched and intoxicated with the fairy dew of the natural magic of the Celt'.

Prospero's last speech in Act IV of *The Tempest* could be an Irish druid on the Hill of Tara communing with the ancient gods. Surely you would have had to have a touch of the Teague to pen a phrase like the one below 'We are such stuff as dreams are made on.'

from THE TEMPEST

These our actors,
As I foretold you, were all spirits, and
Are melted into air, into thin air:
And, like the baseless fabric of this vision,
The cloud-capp'd towers, the gorgeous palaces,
The solemn temples, the great globe itself,
Yea, all which it inherit, shall dissolve;
And, like this insubstantial pageant faded,
Leave not a rack behind. We are such stuff
As dreams are made on, and our little life
Is rounded with a sleep ...

DOUGLAS HYDE
1860-1949

24/01/04

Though this year is the hundredth anniversary of the founding of the Abbey Theatre we have heard little or nothing about the man who wrote the first Abbey play. The fifty-fifth anniversary of Douglas Hyde's death occurs this year. His play was *Casadh an tSugáin* (*The Twisting of the Rope*) and Hyde himself played the leading part. J. M. Synge undoubtedly took the character of his Playboy, Christy Mahon, from Hyde's play, while the rhythms and assonances of Yeats' poems were influenced by Hyde's wonderful translations from the Irish. Michael Collins was another Hyde fan who thought that the founding of the Gaelic League by Hyde was 'the most important event in Ireland in two hundred years'.

Like many of Anglo-Irish background Hyde seemed to be able to excel at anything he tried his hand at. He was the best rifle shot in Connaught, and at Trinity College took four doctorates in Music, Modern Languages, Classical Studies and Divinity. But his translations from Irish poetry are his greatest achievement a sort of miracle of sound in which the internal word music resonates more like an orchestra than a solo instrument.

Douglas Hyde became the first President of Ireland in 1938, inaugurated in St Patrick's Cathedral under the bust of the Irish Protestant patriot Jonathan Swift whom I am sure would have approved.

In the verses below you will see that the last word of one line rhymes with the third or fourth syllable in the next. Say it out loud and keep an ear cocked for the word music.

from I SHALL NOT DIE FOR THEE

For thee I shall not die,
Woman high of fame and name,
Foolish men thou mayest slay,
I and they are not the same.

The round breasts, the fresh skin,
Cheeks crimson, hair like silk to touch,
Indeed, indeed, I shall not die,
Please god, not I, for any such!

Woman, graceful as the swan,
A wise man did rear me, too,
Little palm, white neck, bright eye,
I shall not die for you.

STEPHEN SPENDER
1909-1995

31/01/04

You don't hear much these days of the English poet Stephen Spender who was caught with his hand in the political till, when it was revealed that *Encounter*, the famous literary magazine he edited after the Second World War, was funded by the American Secret Service. It was almost as if the Pope had taken out shares in *Playboy* magazine and Spender, an icon of the Left, somewhat fell from grace. He survived because he was such a decent chap. Though he had fought against Franco in the Spanish Civil War he afterwards generously helped writers who had fought on the other side, such as the South African Roy Campbell who rewarded his benefactor by punching him on the nose.

When I met Spender twenty years ago I was struck by his enormous height (6'4") and eyes, which someone had described as having 'the violent colour of bluebells'. He was a real Londoner, whose Oxford accent, like Evelyn Waugh's, had a slight touch of cockney in it. Appropriately his daughter Lizzie married Dame Edna Everage, Barry Humphreys in real life. In my view Spender's poem 'I Think Continually' ranks among the best written by any English poet of the 1930s.

from I THINK CONTINUALLY

I think continually of those who were truly great.
Who, from the womb, remembered the soul's history
Through corridors of light where the hours are suns
Endless and singing. Whose lovely ambition
Was that their lips, still touched with fire,
Should tell of the Spirit clothed from head to foot in song.
And who hoarded from the Spring branches
The desires falling across their bodies like blossoms.

Near the snow, near the sun, in the highest fields
See how these names are feted by the waving grass
And by the streamers of white cloud
And whispers of wind in the listening sky.
The names of those who in their lives fought for life
Who wore at their hearts the fire's centre.
Born of the sun they travelled a short while towards the sun,
And left the vivid air signed with their honour.

JOHN HENRY NEWMAN
1801-1900

7/02/04

Joyce wrote about Newman 'that nobody has written English prose that can be compared with his'. Sean O'Casey thought Newman was 'as a great a man without his red robe as he was within it' and Elgar, the famous British composer, wrote the music for Newman's *The Dream of Gerontius.*

John Henry Cardinal Newman must have been some guy to have Joyce, O'Casey and Elgar in his fan club. But he had been treated like a fidgety ferret when he came to Dublin in 1854 as Rector of the new Catholic University. The Anglo-Irish detested him as a renegade because of his conversion to Rome, while the Irish bishops bullied him because they feared his Protestant honesty. His biographer Fergal McGrath summed the situation up in a superb simile: '(Cardinal) Cullen and (Archbishop) McHale were like two old country fiddlers playing on the delicate Stradivarius of Newman's temperament.'

Of course the Irish bishops won, and booted the poor man out. But not before he had built the beautiful University Church on Stephen's Green and created the nucleus of a college at 86 Stephen's Green opposite which today, a bust of a former student, James Joyce, stands. In the end, a wise pope made Newman a cardinal, so he could shake his crosier at his enemies but as a true gentleman was not inclined to do so. Here is a lovely hymn written by this priest, poet and writer of powerful prose which today is sung in churches of various faiths throughout the world.

from FACES

LEAD, kindly Light, amid the encircling gloom,
Lead Thou me on;
The night is dark, and I am far from home;
Lead Thou me on.
Keep Thou my feet; I do not ask to see
The distant scene, - one step enough for me.

So long Thy power hath blest me, sure it still
Will lead me on
O'er moor and fen, o'er crag and torrent, till
The night is gone,
And with the morn those angel faces smile,
Which I have loved long since, and lost awhile.

HELEN WADDELL
1889-1965

13/03/03

Before chick-lit arrived we already had a best-selling Irish woman novelist, Helen Waddell from Belfast who in the 1930s wrote *Peter Abelard* which went into seventeen editions. Helen at Oxford had made her name by translating into exquisite verse, the Latin songs of the wandering medieval scholars. Then she went on to write the story of Abelard, the greatest philosopher of the twelfth century known as Rhinoceros Indomitus because he could toss his opponents on the horns of his intellect. When Abelard fell in love with Heloise, his seventeen-year-old pupil, her uncle the Canon of Notre Dame was so infuriated that he took a knife and castrated the famous philosopher. Heloise became a nun, the Abbess of the Paraclete and Abelard survived to write songs about their love that were sung throughout France. It was these songs that Helen Waddell put singing English on for her stunning novel, which by the way is still in print.

from DAVID'S LAMENT FOR JONATHON

Low in the grave with thee
Happy to lie,
Since there's no greater thing left Love to do;
And to live after thee
Is but to die,
For with but half a soul what can Life do?

So share thy victory,
Or else thy grave,
Either to rescue thee, or with thee lie:
Ending that life for thee,
That thou didst save,
So Death that sundereth might bring more nigh.

Peace, O my stricken lute!
Thy strings are sleeping.
Would that my heart could still
Its bitter weeping!

ALFRED NOYES
1880–1958

14/08/04

Alfred Noyes was a stout Staffordshire man who both loved and hated Ireland. He thought we were awful bounders when we arranged the evacuation of his fellow countrymen from here in 1922. But he had a strong streak of honesty which later made him take up the cause of Roger Casement and write a ferocious defence of the Irish patriot's integrity. What he has in common with us is perhaps a love of the sea about which he wrote many poems, one of them of epic length about Sir Francis Drake, the English naval hero. We are after all Europe's only two Atlantic islands harnessed inexorably to the rhythms of that unrelenting tide. The seagulls wheeling over O'Connell Street or waddling down the boulevards in the early morning never let us forget our island heritage.

from SEAGULLS ON THE SERPENTINE
(LONDON)

Memory, out of the mist, in a long slow ripple
 Breaks, blindly, against the shore.
The mist has buried the town in its own oblivion.
 This, this is the sea once more.

Salt in the eyes, and the seagulls, mewing and swooping,
 Snatching the bread from my hand;
Brushing my hand with their breasts, in swift caresses
 To show that they understand.

Oh, why are you so afraid? We are all of us exiles!
 Wheel back in your clamorous rings!
We have all of us lost the sea, and we all remember.
 But you have wings.

SEAN O'CASEY
1880-1964

20/03/04

And where do you leave Sean O'Casey? Certainly in the first five dramatists of the twentieth century. It was he who spotted that working class Dubliners had been speaking poetry all their lives without knowing it and upholstered his plays with their rich language. O'Casey is not known as a poet but any verse that he sneaks into his plays is top class. 'Red Roses for Me' (which is sung in the play of that name) is an almost perfect lyric which could have merited inclusion in Yeats' collection *The Oxford Book of Modern Verse*. Yeats did admire O'Casey's plays immensely and with great courage faced the mob who tried to wreck the Abbey on the first night of *The Plough and the Stars*. 'The fame of O'Casey is born here tonight,' Yeats said standing up with great courage on the stage to face the screaming yobos. 'This is his apotheosis.' O'Casey remarked afterwards that he had to wait until he went home and looked up a dictionary to find out whether Yeats thought him a success or a failure.

from RED ROSES FOR ME

A sober black shawl hides her body entirely,
Touched by the sun and the salt spray of the sea;
But down in the darkness a slim hand so lovely.
Carries a rich bunch of red roses for me.

Her petticoat's simple, her feet are but bare,
An' all that she has on is but neat and scantie;
But stars in the deeps of her eyes are exclaiming
I carry a rich bunch of red roses for thee;

No arrogant gem sits enthroned on her forehead,
Or swings from a white ear for all men to see;
But jewel'd desire in a bosom, most pearly,
Carries a rich bunch of red roses for me.

JOYCE KILMER
1886-1918

19/06/04

A warm summer and the glowing green of the trees unscorched as yet by a relentless sun. Just the time to read Joyce Kilmer's 'Trees'. It is so simply assembled that one might miss the fact that it is a really fine poem as did the compilers of *Chambers Biographical History* who referred to it as 'inexplicably chosen for immortality'. Of course it's inexplicable because if it wasn't we'd all be able to write like that. The fact is, a true poem is one in a million. Kilmer had established his reputation as a poet before joining the American army to fight in France in the last year of the World War I where he was killed in action. He was both male and of Irish descent despite what you might think in coming across his name for the first time.

TREES

I think that I shall never see
A poem lovely as a tree.
A tree whose hungry mouth is prest
Against the earth's sweet flowing breast;
A tree that looks at God all day
And lifts her leafy arms to pray;
A tree that may in summer wear
A nest of robins in her hair;
Upon whose bosom snow has lain;
Who intimately lives with rain
Poems are made by fools like me,
Buy only God can make a tree.

BRENDAN KENNELLY
1936-

17/07/04

Brendan Kennelly ranks among the top living Irish poets. In his early years poems like 'My Dark Fathers' and 'The Blind Man' showed that he had that rarest of gifts, of being able to strike a line, so it can be heard in the mind as you read it. Later he would produce a series of superb translations from the Irish some of them better even than those of his mentor Frank O'Connor.

Poets for some reason tend to be on the small side (Lord Byron, Padraic Colum, James Stephens, Tom Moore, Cahal Ó Searchaigh, to name a few) and because he wasn't in the six foot class, Brendan who was a marvelous catcher and mixer on the All Ireland Kerry minor team, never got a senior jersey. This however gave him time to roam the fields, instead of playing in them, and the result has been splendid verse. I've been nagging Brendan for years to give up the lecture room and turn more to the singing birds in his head. I have heard he may do this soon. If it happens we may then expect 'a startling rout, as of an army driven' in his work, to adapt the phrase used in the poem below.

from THE BIRDS

Beneath the stare of God's gold burning eye,
Two crisp hands clap; a thousand plover rise
And wheel across the meadows of the sky.

Black wings flash and gleam; a perfect white
Makes beautiful each rising breast,
Sovereign in the far-off miracle of flight.

Their terror is a lovely thing,
A sudden inspiration, exploding
In the thunder of each beating wing.

A startling rout, as of an army driven
In broken regiments
Against the proud, fantastic face of heaven.

They breathe on branches, hidden and alone.
Fear will flare again, but now the abandoned sky
Is turning cold and grey as stone.

I think about that marvelous rout, that empty sky,
That flight of plover hidden from
The star of God's gold burning eye.

ELIZABETH BARRETT BROWNING
1806-1861

24/07/04

Last week when two people went to the Oxford Registry Office
to be married, they learned that their favourite poem 'How do
I love Thee' by Elizabeth Barrett Browning couldn't be recited
at the wedding, because it mentioned guess who — God. The
nasty little clerk who decides these things said that under
English law as it stood, civil ceremonies 'must be devoid of
religious content' and produced a whole list of other writers
such as E. M. Forster and Kahlil Gibran whose work is also
forbidden at civil weddings. This censorship by the looney left,
smacks of the Nazi bullies in Germany in the thirties who put a
great deal of effort into humiliating German Jews at every
possible opportunity simply because of their religion and later
some tried to exterminate them. Alas a desire to oppress other
people's views seems to be a facet of human nature. There is a
fascist left just as there a fascist right.

Elizabeth Barrett Browning was married to the poet Robert
Browning and wrote a series of exquisite sonnets which she
translated from the Portuguese. Though she was an invalid it
was a marriage made in heaven as both partners had devoted
their life to create verse which would outlast its time. Here is the
sonnet 'How do I love Thee' which the registrar considered
would have polluted the air of Oxford which Gerard Manley
Hopkins once described as 'towery city and branchy between
towers'.

HOW DO I LOVE THEE

How do I love thee? Let me count the ways.
I love thee to the depth and breadth and height
My soul can reach, when feeling out of sight
For the ends of Being and ideal Grace.
I love thee to the level of everyday's
Most quiet need, by sun and candlelight.
I love thee freely, as men strive for Right;
I love thee purely, as they turn from Praise.
I love thee with the passion put to use
In my old griefs, and with my childhood's faith.
I love thee with a love I seemed to lose
With my lost saints, - I love thee with the breath,
Smiles, tears, of all my life! – and, if God choose,
I shall but love thee better after death.

PATRICK KAVANAGH
1905-1967

7/08/04

Last Saturday week we stood on Baggot Street bridge listening to Peter Kavanagh as he unveiled a plaque to the brother Paddy outside what had been Parson's book shop.

This intense looking man of eighty-nine has devoted a substantial part of his life to keeping the candle of Patrick's genius alight. Undoubtedly his brother's keeper. In the fifties a small community of writers and artists had created here a mini left bank, Baggotonia. In his speech though Peter got his bridges mixed up referring to the one we were standing beside as that over which Paddy had been hurled by his enemies some decades ago. But it was the one further up Leeson Street over which he flew to the accompaniment of a hostile shout, 'That will finish the shagger.'

Luckily he survived to stagger to Patricia Murphy's flat in Wilton Place just across the road where a hot bath and a warm whiskey soon restored him to health.

But it was the canal walk between the two bridges that was Patrick's favourite beat and gave him the setting for his finest sonnet. Read it a few times to get the full flavour. He and Yeats are the two finest Irish poets of the century.

CANAL BANK WALK

Leafy-with-love banks and the green waters of the canal
Pouring redemption for me, that I do
The will of God, wallow in the habitual, the banal,
Grow with nature again as before I grew.
The bright stick trapped, the breeze adding a third
Party to the couple kissing on an old seat,
And a bird gathering materials for the nest for the Word
Eloquently new and abandoned to its delirious beat.
O unworn world enrapture me, enrapture me in a web
Of fabulous grass and eternal voices by a beech,
Feed the gaping need of my senses, give me ad lib
To pray unselfconsciously with overflowing speech
For this soul needs to be honoured with a new dress woven
From green and blue things and arguments that cannot be proven.

WINIFRED M. LETTS
1882-1972

3/07/05

This week sixty-three years ago at an opening night in the Gate Theatre the audience simply didn't know what hit them. The play *Hamilton and Jones* was simply an account of the social and commercial activities of that firm in Dublin from 1886-1936. It was an early example of documentary which worked like a charm because the author Winifred Letts was a poet and novelist who knew how to put a glow on facts. When she was in her eightieth year, her nephew Monk Gibbon (whom she referred to as Willy Monk), brought me to see her in a Dun Laoghaire nursing home. I told her how much I liked her poem 'A Soft Day' which was in the school books at the time, but added that I detested the damn rain, which the poem praised, because it ruined cricket matches and athletic meetings to which I was addicted at the time. She gave a tinkling laugh and said no matter, the important thing was that I liked that poem.

A SOFT DAY

A soft day, thank God!
A wind from the south
With a honeyed mouth;
A scent of drenching leaves,
Briar and beech and lime,
White elder-flower and thyme
And the soaking grass smells sweet,
Crushed by my two bare feet,
While the rain drips,
Drips, drips, drips from the eaves.

A soft day, thank God!
The hills wear a shroud
Of silver cloud;
The web the spider weaves
Is a glittering net;
The woodland path is wet,
And the soaking earth smells sweet
Under my two bare feet,
And the rain drips,
Drips, drips, drips from leaves.

JOHN McCREA
1872-1918

It's autumn and the ninetieth anniversary of the outbreak of the
First World War. It seems now that if the Banger Bush wins the
election in the USA there is a distinct possibility of a third one
getting under way. Those of us who grew up in the period when
survivors of the First World War blinded and crippled were still
to be seen in the streets while a Second World War was being
waged, began to wonder if it was the natural condition of
mankind to seek to kill each other. James Joyce cleverly summed
up the creeping chaos of the period in a letter to a friend

> Any time I turn on the radio I hear some British politician
> mumbling inanities or his German cousin shouting and
> yelling like a madman.

A powerful poem by the Canadian medical officer, Dr John
McCrea, written during the second Battle of Ypres at Flanders
in 1916 carries the message that if we slip once more into world
conflict, we are betraying those who gave their lives to try and
end it.

IN FLANDERS FIELDS

In Flanders Fields the poppies blow
Between the crosses, row on row
That mark our place; and in the sky
The larks, still bravely singing, fly
Scarce heard amid the guns below.

We are the Dead. Short days ago
We lived, felt dawn, saw sunset glow,
Loved and were loved, and now we lie
In Flanders fields.

Take up our quarrel with the foe:
To you from failing hands we throw
The torch; be yours to hold it high.
If ye break faith with us who die
We shall not sleep, though poppies grow
In Flanders fields.

GERARD MANLEY HOPKINS
1844-1889

22/11/03

'I should be glad to see Ireland happy,' Gerard Manley Hopkins wrote in 1887, 'even though it involved the fall of England, if that could come without shame and guilt.' But in 1888 at the age of forty-six this English Jesuit poet died of typhoid in a small room overlooking St Stephen's Green, where he had been part of the teaching staff at University College. It was a serious loss, as Hopkins, who ranks amongst the greatest of English poets, had restored rhythm to poetry. To get the best value from his lines, they should be read aloud to bring up the sound pattern beneath the lines. In 'Spring and Fall: To a Young Child', he makes the point that mourning for the dying years is grieving for oneself.

SPRING AND FALL:
TO A YOUNG CHILD

Margaret, are you grieving
Over Goldengrove unleaving?
Leaves, like the things of man, you
With your fresh thoughts care for, can you?
Ah! As the heart grows older
It will come to such sights colder
By and by now spare a sigh
Though worlds of wanwood leafmeal lie;
And yet you *will* weep and know why.
Now no matter, child, the name:
Sorrow's springs are the same.
Nor mouth had, no nor mind, expressed
What heart heard of, ghost guessed:
It is the blight man was born for,
It is Margaret you mourn for.

ALAN ROSS
1922-2001

22/01/05

Sir Stanley Matthews is held by some to be one of the three great soccer players of all time. On the field he was like a phantom. His body seemed to dissolve as he went at his opponent and then appeared on the other side with the ball, as if he had gone through him. He played first division football for Stoke until he was over fifty. I had seen him work his magic at Dalymount Park and was later lucky enough to play there on the wing against him in 1969 for a selected Old Irish eleven against Old England. In the second half Matthews went through four players like a knife through butter after changing from the right to the left wing, because in the first half Peter Farrell (Everton), Liam Tuohy (Newcastle), and myself had formed a ring around him every time he got the ball.

In a poem written about Sir Stanley, Alan Ross brings before the mind's eye a picture of this marvelous man with the ball at his feet creating a choreography comparable to the Veronica, a bullfighter achieves with his cape.

from STANLEY MATTHEWS

At last, unrefusable, dangling the ball at the instep
He is charged – and stiffening so slowly
It is rarely perceptible, he executes with a squirm
Of the hips, a twist more suggestive than apparent,
That lazily disdainful move toreros term
A Veronica – it's enough.

Only emptiness following him, pursuing some scent
Of his own, he weaves in towards,
Not away from, fresh tacklers,
Who, turning about to gain time, are by him
Harried, pursued not pursuers.

Expressionless enchanter, weaving as on strings
Conceptual patterns to a private music, heard
Only by him, to whose slowly emerging theme
He rehearses steps, soloist in compulsions of a dream.

PATRICK KAVANAGH
1905-1967

I got a real kick when Patrick Kavanagh approved my first book. It wasn't easy to squeeze praise out of him. Ferociously cranky he could be. Once when a girl, Beverly McNamara, came up to him in McDaid's with a little too much makeup on her he refused to buy her a drink.

'Do you not see I have a mouth on me?' she said

'How could I miss it and it swinging between your two ears like a skipping rope?

He really did love Hilda Moriarity though to whom the poem below is addressed. Bob Bradshaw the best talker in McDaid's described her well when he said she had 'eyes like burning coals at the bottom of a shaft which you could put your two fingers into'. She turned Paddy down and he never really got over it. He told me how he found out. One day he'd passed a cinema queue on O'Connell street and there she was standing with a Dublin solicitor. 'I went up to O'Connell bridge and I spat into the river'.

But it's hung on such cliffs of loneliness that poets can find their best inspiration. Out of this experience Patrick got 'Raglan Road': that rare creation a true ballad. He'd heard the real thing so often in his boyhood, when he came to write in this form about his own experience he made a miraculous blend between the two.

RAGLAN ROAD

On Raglan Road on an autumn day I met her first and knew
That her dark hair would weave a snare that I might one day rue;
I saw the danger, yet I walked along the enchanted way,
And I said, let grief be a fallen leaf at the dawning of the day.

On Grafton Street in November we tripped lightly along the ledge
Of the deep ravine where can be seen the worth of passion's pledge,
The Queen of Hearts still making tarts and I not making hay –
O I loved too much and by such by such is happiness thrown away.

I gave her gifts of the mind I gave her the secret sign that's known
To the artists who have known the true gods of sound and stone
And word and tint. I did not stint for I gave her poems to say
With her own name there and her own dark hair like clouds over fields of May.

On a quiet street where old ghosts meet I see her walking now
Away from me so hurriedly my reason must allow
That I had wooed not as I should a creature made of clay –
When the angel woos the clay he'd lose his wings at the dawn of day.

OLIVER ST JOHN GOGARTY
1878-1957

19/10/04

Ringsend Strand or the *Waxies Dargle* as it was known to Dubliners has had a big clean up, and the beach has many visitors these warm autumn days. Forty years ago it was packed every summer with Dublin mothers and their families from the inner city who brought their children out to the beautiful beach on the number two tram and had picnics there with sandwiches and tea brewed on primus stoves. Mornings were enlivened by the great Shakespearean actor Anew McMaster running from his house across Strand Road in his bathing togs and diving clean over the wall head first into the sea. Mr de Valera used to walk two miles every morning on Sandymount Strand on his way to work while Oliver St John Gogarty, the poet, kept a horse in a nearby stable for his morning ride on the golden stretch, which he commemorated in a famous poem which you will find in the *Oxford Book of Modern Verse*.

RINGSEND

I will live in Ringsend
With a red-headed whore,
And the fan-light gone in
Where it lights the hall-door;
And listen each night
For her querulous shout,
As at last she streels in
And the pubs empty out.
To soothe that wild breast
With my old-fangled songs,
Till she feels it redressed
From inordinate wrongs,
Imagined, outrageous,
Preposterous wrongs,
Till peace at last comes,
Shall be all I will do,
Where the little lamp blooms
Like a rose in the stew;
And up the back-garden
The sounds come to me
Of the lapsing, unsoilable,
Whispering sea.

FRANCIS STUART
1902-2000

4/06/05

This is the fifth anniversary of the death of Francis Stuart who lived to be ninety-eight years of age. Three of his novels rank him as one of the important writers of the twentieth century. He wrote fine poetry too but would say 'I'm addicted to prose'. A poem of his, 'Night Pilot', is however in my view, one of the best poems yet written to represent the poet's function in society. In 'Night Pilot' the poem starts with a wonderfully evocative description of a plane taking off and landing. But the true voyage takes place on land when the poet will fly rudderless on the wings of his imagination into the unknown. From his small house he will have earned an outlet to runways, which are the preserve of the poet without radar and at risk.

NIGHT PILOT

The journey's getting longer every flight,
The black clouds blacker in their fringe of ice,
And in his ears the mariner's tolling bell
Of warning to the shuddering carapace
That earth looms up beneath the fragile shell.
The robot gadget landing blind and well
And he ever impatient to be gone
To the small house in which he is a guest
And whence lead half the runways of the globe,
But where he is without automaton
To ease the anguish of his inner probe,
Take on the risk and burden of his quest.

JAMES ELROY FLECKER
1884-1915

This year is the ninetieth anniversary of James Elroy Flecker's death who wrote one of my favorite poems of all time, 'The Old Ships'. Of course Flecker wrote other fine verse and was the author of *Hassan,* one of the few successful full-length verse dramas of the twentieth century. But 'The Old Ships' takes the biscuit.

How often lying on the strand has one's eye been caught by a white sail scudding across the blue. It was from such a moment on a Mediterranean beach that Flecker created the scene which sends the mind racing back in time. The first line of the poem is magic: 'I have seen old ships sail like swans asleep.'

The sails nestled on their blue bedspread set the poet thinking of how often the ships would have had to hoist sail to escape the pirates who roamed the Mediterranean sea. Stretching his mind he wonders was this the ship that bore Ulysses and his comrades away from the burning of Troy. In the true spirit of Homer he doesn't romanticise the hero, but sees him as a 'talkative bald-headed seaman', even a bore going on about his exploits.

THE OLD SHIPS

I have seen old ships sail like swans asleep
Beyond the village which men still call Tyre,
With leaden age o'ercargoed, dipping deep
For Famagusta and the hidden sun
That rings black Cyprus with a lake of fire;
And all those ships were certainly so old
Who knows how oft with squat and noisy gun,
Questing brown slaves or Syrian oranges,
The pirate Genoese
Hell-raked them till they rolled
Blood, water, fruit and corpses up the hold.
But now through friendly seas they softly run,
Painted the mid-sea blue or shore-sea green,
Still patterned with the vine and grapes in gold.

But I have seen,
Pointing her shapely shadows from the dawn
An image tumbled on a rose-swept bay,
A drowsy ship of some yet older day;
And, wonder's breath indrawn,
Thought I – who knows-who knows-but in that same
(Fished up beyond Aeaea, patched up new
-Stern painted brighter blue-)
That talkative, bald-headed seaman came
(Twelve patient comrades sweating at the oar)
From Troy's doom-crimson shore,
And with great lies about his wooden horse
Set the crew laughing, and forgot his course.

It was so old a ship- who knows, who knows?
-And yet so beautiful, I watched in vain
To see the mast burst open with a rose,
And the whole deck put on its leaves again.

175

SEAMUS HEANEY
1939-

For a small country our literary record is impressive. Four
Irishmen have won the Nobel Prize for Literature, three
Dubliners (the only city anywhere to achieve this) and a Derry
man. Beckett, Shaw and Yeats can be regarded as city guys. But
Seamus Heaney is from Derry farming stock, the same breed
which fifteen hundred years ago produced Columcille the first
poet to popularise rhyme in Latin verse.

My favorite Heaney poem is 'The Diviner' in which he deals
with the almost magic power a few have, to discover with a
hazel stick, water beneath the earth. Take the last three words
of the poem 'The hazel stirred'. On their own nothing out of
the ordinary. But harnessed by Heaney to his rhythmic score
they come over with an orchestral crash — almost making us
feel running through our own arms the current received by the
diviner himself.

THE DIVINER

Cut from the green hedge a forked hazel stick
That he held tight by the arms of the V:
Circling the terrain, hunting the pluck
Of water, nervous, but professionally

Unfussed. The pluck came sharp as a sting.
The rod jerked with precise convulsions,
Spring water suddenly broadcasting
Through a green hazel its secret stations.

The bystanders would ask to have a try.
He handed them the rod without a word.
It lay dead in their grasp till, nonchalantly,
He gripped expectant wrists. The hazel stirred.

ALLEN GINSBERG
1926-1997

Allen Ginsberg, poetry icon of the Beats was a twentieth century messiah in a three-piece suit. The son of a doctor he never quite lost the sharp clinical look under his towering whiskers. When I met him at the last Beat public presentation on 17 April 1971 in the Macmillan Hall, New York, the first thing he asked me was had his work been banned by the censorship board in Ireland. I told him neither he nor Joyce were banned but Graham Greene was, and he seemed almost disappointed. Leave it to the Irish!

Ginsberg left a vast body of verse behind (almost twice as big as Yeats) but a lot of it varies in quality. His most famous poem is a long one the marvelous 'Howl' which catches the voice of a new generation who felt the need to shake off what they regarded as an outdated morality. It's written in the rhythm which Ginsberg took from Walt Whitman and adapted to the tune of the jazz age. 'The endless ride from Battery to Holy Bronx' refers to a sixties custom of spending the night on the subway train zonked up, until eventually morning came and the train would end its last night run after it passed the Zoo.

from HOWL

I saw the best minds of my generation destroyed by madness,
starving hysterical naked,
dragging themselves through the Negro streets at dawn looking
for an angry fix,
angleheaded hipsters burning for the ancient heavenly
connection to the starry dynamo in the machinery of night, ...
who chained themselves to subways for the endless ride from
Battery to holy Bronx on Benzedrine until the noise of
wheels and children brought them down shuddering
mouth-wracked and battered bleak of brain all drained
of brilliance on the drear light of Zoo, ...
and rose reincarnate in the ghostly clothes of jazz in the
goldhorn shadow
of the band and blew the suffering of America's naked mind
for love into a saxophone cry ... that shivered the cities down
to the last radio.
with the absolute heart of the poem of life butchered out of
their own bodies good to eat a thousand years.

W. B. YEATS
1866-1939

28/05/05

Anne Gregory was the granddaughter of Lady Gregory, one of the founders of the Abbey Theatre, and was brought up by her at Coole House in Galway before she went away to school. All the literary heavyweights used to visit there: Sean O'Casey, George Bernard Shaw and the poet Yeats. The latter was captivated by Ann. 'She has hair like a cornfield,' he announced, and wrote a wonderful poem about her. When Yeats read the poem at tea one evening, Ann aged six was not overly impressed. She felt the poem was 'very doggerly and not as romantic as I would have liked'. Later when she heard the poet reading it on the BBC she recognised that she had been commemorated in a masterpiece. Her enthusiasm was somewhat deflated the next day, however, when she got a note from a boyfriend containing this verse

If I was alone on an island

And only Ann with me there.

I'd make myself cushions to sleep on

By stuffing her skin with her hair.

FOR ANNE GREGORY

'Never shall a young man,
Thrown into despair
By those great honey-coloured
Ramparts at your ear,
Love you for yourself alone
And not your yellow hair.'

'But I can get a hair-dye
And set such colour there,
Brown, or black, or carrot,
That young men in despair
May love me for myself alone
And not my yellow hair.'

'I heard an old religious man
But yesternight declare
That he had found a text to prove
That only God, my dear,
Could love you for yourself alone
And not your yellow hair.'

COPYRIGHT PERMISSIONS